The Fall of Christendom and the Separation of the Remnant

Are you part of the remnant?

Frank McEleny

DEDICATION

This book is dedicated to all the saints of every age who have counted the cost and willingly paid the price.

CONTENTS

ACKNOWLEDGMENTS

I would like to thank a dear brother in Christ who contributed chapters 5, 6&7 of this book. I would also like to acknowledge all the saints in the world who love the Truth and will stand upon it no matter what happens in their lives.

1.

WHAT DOES THE WORD REMNANT MEAN IN THE CONTEXT OF OUR DAY?

I would like to clarify what I mean when I use the term "remnant". To use any word over and over again can make it take on a life of its own. A remnant child of God is simply someone who genuinely knows Jesus, someone who has been truly converted. Now, why the distinction, why even use any other name rather than simply "Christian?" Well, I am certainly not stuck on the name, to me it is more of an adjective than a noun. It simply describes what Jesus was talking about when He says "many are called, but few are chosen."(Matt 22:14) Now, just as that was true when Jesus spoke it, it is equally true now. The context of that scripture comes from the previous chapter when Jesus showed that men would not give to God what was rightfully His, instead they rejected and killed His son. Now in chapter 22 Jesus uses another illustration, this time a wedding, which people were too busy to come to.

So, Jesus establishes that the invitation is there before men to give to God what is His, to come when invited, but by and large they reject this and only a relatively small number accept. This same invitation exists today. Now, let us look at the name Christian. In a western world that by and large calls itself Christian by name and by birth, then we have to have a further distinction because we know that simply being born into a "Christian" household does not make one a Christian. Neither does calling one-self a Christian make that person a Christian. There needs to be a genuine conversion, a new creature in Christ, a new birth actually and not merely theologically and of course there are marks of this new birth. Now, C.S. Lewis, more than half a century ago, wrote about the fact that the term

"Christian" had lost its meaning. He used the word "Gentleman" to illustrate what he meant.

More than three hundred years ago, in England, the term "Gentleman" meant that one was a landowner. If you did not own land, you were not a Gentleman. Now, over the following decades and centuries, whether men owned land or not, they began to call themselves Gentlemen, thus emptying the actual meaning of the word. Lewis was arguing that this was exactly what has happened to the word "Christian." I agree entirely with Lewis and of course things have not improved in the last 50 years. And so the definition of the word remnant is, as a noun, "a small remaining quantity of something." As an adjective "remaining." Webster's defines the word to mean "a small surviving group." Now, if 7000 did not bow the knee to Baal and there was roughly a population of seven million in that day, that means that for every one thousand people, only one had not bowed the knee to Baal.

If we extrapolated that number to today, that would mean there were just over three million in the USA who had not bowed their knees to the gods of today. I am not suggesting such a low number, I personally think it is much higher than that, but you get the idea. And so, as we move on down through the centuries from Pentecost, we begin to see a religious kingdom built by men who believed they were doing the work of God, for the most part this kingdom was the kingdom of Catholicism. This is what I would call "Christendom." The world of Christendom is everything that calls itself Christian. Yet, only a relatively small number stood against the heretical teachings of the Catholic Church down through the ages. We now know them as martyrs, but in their day they were known as heretics by Christendom.

You can read about these people in many different publications, Foxes Book of Martyrs is an excellent resource as is "The Pilgrim Church." And so, in all of those ages, including the dark ages God had a witness, God had His Church and the gates of hell could not prevail against it, even although they came at it with all of hell's fury. Now, as it was then so it is today. Christendom is by and large made up of a religious people who have not been genuinely born again. And just as there are marks of those who have been born again, obviously those who have not will have their own marks, the marks of the world. And of course we see that in divorce rates and so on that is no different, and in some cases higher than the world. And so, while there are baby Christians and mature Christians and weaker Christians and everything in between in genuine Christianity, this makes up the population of the Church because the one thing they will all have in common is that they have had a genuine conversion experience as opposed to having been merely born into a Christian family or made a confession of faith or signed on a dotted line at some time.

Well, if this has always been the case and today is just the same really then why is there any urgency in the genuine Church? Well, I believe it is because of the prophetic calendar. And by that I mean that so many in God's Body believe that the return of the Lord is coming soon, perhaps even in our own lifetime. Now one may argue that Christians have always thought that. I would argue that without the return of Israel and other prophecies then the prophetic clock could never really have begun to come close to the time we are now approaching. And what time is that? Well since I do not believe in a pre-trib rapture, nor do I believe in Dominionism, then I believe that the birth pangs have begun and there is a count-down to the time of severe persecution. A persecution so bad that if the Lord did not shorten those days then

Frank McEleny

there would simply be no genuine Christians left alive prior to the return of Jesus. Now with persecution I will argue that the Lord will pour out His Spirit on His people in order for them to be equipped to handle such times.

And because the persecution will be so severe, then the Spirit will be poured out as has never been seen before, in essence, the glory of the Lord will cover the earth as the waters cover the sea because persecution will be worldwide. Now, this takes us back to the remnant children, simply the genuinely converted. As the denominations and churches continue their slide into compromise and apostasy, it will become increasingly difficult for genuine believers to stay where they are. And, when you add to that scenario the removing of God's presence from these churches, it will simply become intolerable for genuine Christians to stay in these places. They will begin to come out, and have been coming out for quite some-time. As the light begins to be removed from these churches by the removal of the light-bearers, the genuine Christians, then the denominations and dead churches will more and more identify with the world and with the State. This will set them up to become part of a World church and at the same time set them up to eventually become the deadliest enemies of the genuine Christian who cannot and will not stand by and be part of an ever sliding, ever darkening compromising establishment.

Yet, the genuine Christian has always loved his genuine brothers and sisters and loves too fellowship with like-minded passionate Spirit filled believers. And so they will find each other and as the end of ages approaches, they will comfort and encourage one another. Brothers and sisters, we are living in these times right now. Now it may be the beginning of the process, but the process, the great falling away is already well under way and is setting the stage for what is to come. In our lifetime? Very possibly. Our children or grandchildren's lifetime? Almost certainly. Yet saints, even if it were 100 years off (which I do not believe) God would already be preparing His children for the end of the age. Now more than ever we must be able to hear that small still voice and know the Word of God. Now more than ever we must cherish the genuine presence of God in the midst of so much counterfeit. Stay

10

close to the Lord and look for His lead and follow His directions. Hold the things of this world loosely (as we should always do anyway) and trust in Him and lean not on your own understanding.

2.

THE PURPOSE OF THE REMNANT CHURCH IN OUR DAY.

Remnant church is, at its core and most fundamentally, God's witness here on earth. Truly we have been called first and foremost to be a witness. Now most saints know that this word in its Greek form translates to martyr. Does that mean that every saint, every witness since the beginning of the church has been called to martyrdom? Certainly not. Yet let us not forget brothers and sisters that in every century God's people here on earth have been persecuted and martyred for their faith. The danger for the saints in the Western world in the last couple of hundred years is that we have not had to face such trials. Other saints around the world cannot say that, whether that is Africa or Asia or China or the Middle East, they have continued to be persecuted and martyred for their faith. For most of Europe and North America, this has not been the case.

Now, one would imagine that living in an atmosphere where one is allowed to worship freely without any state or religious interference that Christendom would thrive. Yet if we look at the state of Europe and North America we see something that at best, is a shallow faith. In the case of Europe we definitely see a post Christian society. In North America what is predominant is a cultural Christianity, a cross-less Christianity and a Christ-less Christianity. Cultural Christianity would be a Christianity that is simply shaped to suit our culture. In this kind of Christianity Jesus would rarely be mentioned and God would be seen as some kind of Santa Claus. A cross-less Christianity would cover movements like the prosperity gospel, name it and claim it groups, Word of faith believers and health and wealth believers. Or again, a hybrid of all three. A Christ less Christianity would cover dead denominations for whom the Word of God has ceased to be authoritative even in pretense and where all things are acceptable, this would include things like gay marriage and gay ministers, abortion, divorce and so on.

Now what does the genuine saint look like, what does the true witness look like? Consider this passage from the book "The Pilgrim Church" *They have drunk of the water that flows from the Sanctuary of God, from the Well of Life, and from this have obtained a heart that cannot be comprehended by human mind or understanding. They have found that God helped them to bear the cross and they have overcome the bitterness of death. The fire of God burned in them. Their tabernacle was not here on the earth but was pitched in Eternity, and they had foundation and certainty for their faith. Their faith blossomed as a lily, their faithfulness as a rose, their piety and uprightness as flowers of God's planting.*

The Angel of the Lord had swung his spear before them , so that the helmet of salvation, the golden shield of David, could not be wrested from them. They have heard the horn blown in Sion and have understood it and on that account they have cast down all pain and martyrdom and not feared. Their Holy temper counted the things valued by the world as a shadow, knowing greater things. They were trained by God, so that they knew nothing, sought nothing, willed nothing, loved nothing, but the eternal heavenly Good only. Therefore they had more patience in their sufferings than their enemies in inflicting them." (The Pilgrim Church)

The Remnant man or woman carries their cross. Carrying a cross is a lonely business. It's their very loneliness that compels them to seek an even closer walk with the Lord. The trials of the cross is the way of the remnant saint. The narrowness of the path, the desert and wilderness that often stretches out before them is a way of life. A lack of fitting in is their lot but the remnant saint only seeks to see the Lord high and lifted up. You will often despair at your own walk even although people tell you what a great man or woman of God you are, you hear that and it makes you cringe because you know how far you fall short of a God that you have seen high and lifted up. You continually seek Him, you live for the next encounter with Him. You know that it is only a moment but there will come a time when it will be an eternity. You long for everyone to radically encounter the Living God for themselves. You hear people say that they would like your anointing and you wonder. You wonder if they could walk through the refining fires of the living God. Would they really want their whole lives dismantled piece by piece? Would they like the bread of adversity and the waters of afflictions to be their teachers? God's Remnant people walk this path.

The remnant know that just as the world hated their Lord and crucified Him, they too will be hated and killed all the day long for His names sake. And just as He arose, they know that they too will arise. As they draw nearer to "the one who was pierced," and He pours out His Spirit on them and they become more like Him, then the same forces that came against their Jesus, hell and all its fury, will come against them. They know that "unless a grain of wheat falls to the ground and dies, it abides alone, but if it dies it brings forth much fruit."

The Remnant saint knows something of the glory of God. He has been touched by it, ruined for the things of this word by it. He has a fire that burns in his bones that will not and cannot be quenched. He is single-minded in his devotion. He arises in the morning with thoughts of His Lord. He walks through the day thinking about His Lord and communing with Him. He ever lives to serve His God. He knows he falls short but continues on, continues to pursue. He is relentless in his pursuit of God, he is diligent to walk worthily before His Lord for His Lord is not a God that dwells in a lofty ivory tower who cannot be touched.

His Lord and his God dwells within his very heart and he walks with him daily and his heart burns within him. Those who have experienced the glory of God walk in victory. It is this victory that allows for joy even in the midst of suffering. For those who walk in the presence of God, who have seen the glory of God in the face of Jesus cannot help but radiate His glory. It is not something that is achieved. If the remnant saint radiates joy it's because he is like the moon. The moon is a dead object, yet the light of the sun reflects off the moon and lights up a dark world. And just as the moon, by virtue of its position to the sun and the earth, radiates the light down into the darkness, then so to do those Christians who come before the throne and kneel before the King, They radiate the light from this glorious place into the darkness of the world. Yet while the remnant saint is dead to the world, he is alive to his Christ and Lord.

All of the above mentioned virtues of the remnant saints makes them a deadly enemy of the adversary. And the adversary, through his proxy's, has and does and will continue to attack them relentlessly in any way that he can. The particular enemy of the remnant saint is not the world, it's the religious man. Every part of the remnant saint's walk exposes the religious man for who and what he is. Fundamentally the religious man is a man who knows nothing of the Lord. The religious man has head knowledge for sure. He typically has position in life. He is typically political. He cares for the things of this world. He cares about himself and his own. He cares for his reputation. At his core he is an enemy of the cross of Christ. Not Christ Himself, for he loves the notion of Christ and would never deny the fundamental doctrines for he is at his core very orthodox but he is as Paul describes…. *"For many are walking, of whom I have told you often and now tell you weeping, as the enemies of the cross of Christ, whose end is destruction, whose god is their belly, and whose glory is in their shame, those who mind earthly things."* (Phil 3:18-19)

You see a religious man would never willingly suffer. The notion of suffering and sacrifice to the religious man is an abhorrent one. This is a spirit that has existed almost from the beginning. We see it in Cain and Abel. Abel's sacrifice was acceptable to God. Fire always falls on sacrifice. The fire of God's Spirit falls upon what is acceptable to God. Cain realizes this and hates his brother and kills his brother. We see it in David and Saul. We see Saul taking up the spear and trying to pin David to the wall. Yet all David was doing was worshipping the Lord and undoubtedly experiencing the presence and favor of God. Saul knew this and hated it and hunted him down with ruthlessness and with violence. We further see it with the Pharisees and the Sadducees and their scribes. These two groups of people who were religious and political enemies, came together in common purpose, along with the crowd and with zealots to do away with Jesus. Better Jesus to die and them to keep their positions and save their own necks. And after all, had not Jesus exposed them as hypocrites?

3.

THOSE WHO HATE THE REMNANT SAINTS.

The Romans hated the remnant believers because they would not bow their knee to the gods of this world. And because of this they poured out great fury and destruction against the saints. And then we see the Catholic Church take up the same cause, for the saints would not bow their knee to any Pope or false doctrine. The saints would rather suffer death than live a compromised religious life. Now why would they do this? Was it because they had some alternative religion or philosophy? No, these saints had "tasted," of the heavenly gifts. They had been touched by the glory of God. It burned in their very souls. They, like Paul, could say that whatever things were gain to them that they would count it as loss for Christ. In fact they too would count all things loss for the excellency of the knowledge of Christ Jesus. Now this "knowledge" was not a head knowledge but was an intimate word. Scripture tells us that Joseph did not "know" Mary until after Jesus was born. It is this sense of "knowing" that is related to here, not a physical intimacy but a spiritual one which is actually much deeper than any physical union. We are one in Christ actually, not theologically. The remnant saints have this "knowledge." This is why they were and are willing to give up everything, to count all things as loss and rubbish so that they can be found "in Christ," and that they may "know Him."

And so we can see that in every age and in every century, the real saint, the remnant saint, the saint that has not bowed his knee to the gods of this world, is the deadly enemy of the religious man. In every century they have hunted him down and killed him. And now we are approaching the end of the ages. The forces that have lain dormant in the west in regard to persecuting the saints to any great degree have not gone away. The spirits behind this persecution simply lay in wait for the right time. And now, with our Lord coming back soon, their time is short. The prophetic calendar has a mighty role to play in what is to unfold shortly. If you can accept that the Lord is coming back soon, then you must accept that the anti-Christ will soon rise. In 2 Th 2:3 it says *"Let not anyone deceive you by any means, for that day shall not come unless first comes a falling away, and the man of sin shall be revealed, the son of perdition, who opposes and exalts himself above all that is called God."*

So we know that when Scripture warns us not to be deceived, that there is a great propensity to be deceived and so we must be careful. There must first come a great falling away. I would like to argue brothers and sisters that this great falling away has taken place before our very eyes and is unfolding as you read this. Christendom in Europe is all but dead. A mere 3% of British people go to church and the numbers in Europe, excluding Catholics is no better. We have previously described the state of Christianity in North America as mostly cultural, cross-less and Christ-less. And it is precisely because of this great falling away that the remnant saints are coming out, separating themselves, from what passes as Christendom.

As the process of the falling away deepens and speeds up, and as wrong becomes more and more acceptable and actually becomes right to the religious, then more and more remnant saints will separate themselves from what is now known as Christendom. This separating is not a call by men but it is a call from God. God is calling His people out of the deadness of denominationalism. It is vital and necessary because God always has a witness on the earth. As the days darken and become more and more like the days of Noah and as the remnant believers come out in greater numbers, then God will begin to pour out His Spirit more and more on His saints as they begin to dwell in unity and love one another. And the more anointed God's remnant saints become, then the greater the persecution becomes.

God's remnant people stand in direct opposition to the cultural winds that blow. And the more of a witness that they are, the more that their light shines in the darkness then the more of a threat they become. Scripture warns us of a great whore church that will arise in the end times. What will be the makeup of this great whore church and how will it operate? Well we know that war is made upon the saints and this war will be led by the whore church at the behest of its leader. The antichrist will have come initially as a man of peace, he will in all likelihood save the world from imminent disaster or post disaster. He will unite Christendom, Islam and Judaism. Now brothers and sisters, as preposterous as this seems now, can I tell you that we can already see the building blocks of this being put in place, stepping-stones if you like. Even today we see movements such as "Chrislam" led by dead denominations devoid of the Spirit and of truth where they have joint services with Muslims. We also know that Dispensationalism, which is much broader than you may know and in fact carries a majority position within Christendom in matters relating to end times, has a radical position within its movement. This position in regards to Israel allows them to have joint services with Jewish people. And so even today, we see the beginnings of the great whore church that will encompass the world's great religions.

Dispensationalism is also one of the biggest proponents of a pre-trib rapture so they could never accept what we are speaking of here without jettisoning their fundamental doctrines. And so, religious people, united under one god, led by the antichrist and the false prophet and with the support of the world/state will ruthlessly and with an ancient spirit come against every saint across the planet. In every tribe and every tongue and every nation the saints of God, the remnant saints who refuse to bow down to this god will be persecuted and imprisoned and killed like lambs to the slaughter. Will this be our generation or a generation soon to come? No one knows, but it will, in relative terms, be soon. The Bridegroom is coming soon for His Bride. It is time to ready ourselves for what is to come.

There is much said about preparation in the Scriptures. And so we must prepare ourselves. The essence of preparedness can be seen and is highlighted at Gethsemane. This is where the battle of Calvary was truly won. Jesus fought the battle on His knees and by His obedience and willingness to embrace the will of His Father. This is where we too will prepare and will win the battle before it is even fought. It will be on our knees, and with an overwhelming desire to carry out the Lord's will for our lives, even if it means actual martyrdom. We must be willing to embrace our God who could call us to martyrdom. We must be willing to embrace the cross and all that it means. It is vital to remember that the wrath the Lord saved us from is the wrath of eternal damnation, not the wrath of men who will persecute us and kill us. Some modern-day Christians would have you believe that because Jesus suffered and died for us then we will not have to suffer and possibly die for Him. This is preposterous and is in direct violation of countless Scriptures. And not only that, we have nineteen centuries of our brothers and sisters, starting with the apostles, suffering, being persecuted and dying for the cause of Christ.

Brothers and sisters, this upcoming time of persecution and end of ages is not something to be feared. Yes, in the natural it would be, but God's saints do not operate in the natural. They know from experience that perfect love casts out all fear. They know that they have not been given a spirit of fear. They know that the Lord will never leave them nor forsake them. They know that even as the enemy comes in like a flood that God Himself will raise up a standard. Now what is a standard? A standard is a flag. A standard-bearer in times of war is a carrier of a flag and leads the way into battle. A flag denotes oneness and unity. Our flag, our standard, our unity is that we are one in Christ, united in His sufferings and sharers of His glory, the glory that was given to Him by His Father. This glory will only increase as the darkness increases. For even a small candle gives off a great light in total darkness, yet we do not have a small light burning in us brothers and sisters we have a mighty flame.

We have been baptized in the Holy Spirit and in fire. The same fire that lit up the desert night sky and led the children of Israel through the wilderness, also lights up and illuminates our path brothers and sisters, only now the fire is within is and we are the light of the world for Christ Himself dwells within us. Do not be afraid of things to come, do not be afraid of the gathering storm. Simply let your light so shine before men and keep your eyes on Jesus. This light that you have is part of the glorious light of eternity for it is the very light of Christ Himself that burns in us. We have glimpsed eternity saints. We "know" something of it. We have tasted of the heavenly gifts. We have been partakers of the Holy Spirit, we have been ruined for the things of this world because of these glimpses.

Keep your eyes on Jesus and your mind on things eternal. This will allow you to praise the Lord your God in everything and give thanks. For because of your eternal mind-set you will know that nothing will separate you from the love of Jesus. Persecution cannot separate us, trials and tribulations cannot separate us, those who seek to kill us and death cannot separate us from the love of Jesus for we know that for His sake we are killed all the day long and that we are counted as sheep for the slaughter. We know this because we know Jesus and we know His Word. We also know that in all of these things we are more than conquerors in Christ Jesus because of His great love for us. And so brothers and sisters "I am persuaded that neither death nor life, nor angels nor principalities, nor powers, nor things present, nor things to come, nor heights nor depths, nor any other creature shall be able to separate us from the love of God which is in Christ Jesus." Look forward saints, look upwards and cast your spiritual eyes unto things eternal, and you will overcome because he is your Lord and Savior Jesus and your eternal reward will be to dwell with Him. There is nothing in this world that is worth more than this.

4.

WILL YOU OVERCOME?

If I were to simply ask the question "what does it mean to overcome?" I am sure I would get many different answers. The word "overcomer," in the Greek means to *"Conquer, to subdue, to prevail and to get the victory."* Now if one is earthly minded and walked with the notion that we have been called to live our best life now, one might believe that to overcome is to have victory over the circumstances of our lives. This may include health issues or wealth issues. So to those who believe in that way, overcoming would mean getting a healing when one is sick. Or, if one is dying then being delivered from death. It could also mean that if one is poor, then by becoming rich one has overcome their poverty.

Now, does God heal? Yes He does. Can He raise a man from his deathbed, or raise the dead? Yes of course. Can he take a poor man and raise him up to walk with kings? Yes He can and has often done so. Are any of these formulas whereby God must act? No. God alone chooses who he raises up, whether it is from poverty or from a bed of sickness or a bed of death or even death itself and He does it for His own will and His own good pleasure. One can definitely say that all these things can be overcome according to the will of God. Yet that is an entirely different subject, I am interested in the over-comers of the first three chapters of Revelation. Who are they? There are three classic interpretations of who the overcomers are, let me just list them and I want you to think as you read these three versions what you believe. Maybe you have never thought about it before? Overcomers are those who persevere by obedience and are victorious in the face of trials and to whom all the promises of Jesus pertain to, so who are they and will you be one of them? ....

1. The promises are experienced by all believers who are genuinely saved and therefore overcome, and those who do not overcome were never genuinely saved in the first place.

2. The promises are experienced by all genuine believers who overcome and if you do not overcome then you lose your salvation.

3. Promises are experienced by faithful and obedient believers who overcome, and those who fail to overcome, while still genuine believers, lose their rewards while maintaining their salvation.

The third option is the one most commonly held to in this day of Christianity. Yet, if we actually look at what Jesus says would we really come to that conclusion. Let us look at what some of what Jesus says to the churches.

PROMISES TO THOSE WHO OVERCOME; New name, fed by hidden manna, rise up and reign with Christ, walk with Jesus, clothed with white, name written in the book of life and Jesus will confess our names before His Father. A living vital part of the temple,

TO THOSE WHO DO NOT OVERCOME; No new name, not fed, no reigning with Christ, walk alone, naked, wretched, spewed out of the Lords mouth, name blotted out of the book of life, Jesus will be ashamed of them before His Father

When you read the promises side by side with the warnings and the results of failure to overcome it becomes quite stark. This overcoming that Jesus speaks of is the difference between life and death, eternal life and death. Now while all of the issues that Jesus spoke of to the Churches have always had personal and corporate application, it also has an end time application. Overcoming in this context has nothing to do with the issues we spoke of at the start of this article. For example, to the Church of Smyrna, an impoverished church already facing many trials, Jesus warns that they are about to have more tribulations and they will be thrown into prison. Jesus commends them to be faithful unto death. You see, overcoming in this situation had nothing to do with alleviating their immediate circumstances, in fact quite the opposite.

Over-comers can say with Job in 13:15 *Even though He kills me yet will I trust in Him and I will maintain my ways before Him.* Job was an overcomer. The three Hebrew children were overcomers because no matter their circumstances they would not bow down to any golden image and were more concerned about honoring their God than any king of this world.

Dan 3:17 *If it be so, our God whom we serve is able to deliver us from the burning fiery furnace, and he will deliver us out of thine hand, O king .But if not, be it known unto thee, O king, that we will not serve thy gods, nor worship the golden image which thou hast set up.*

These Hebrew children were overcomers and in this spirit the Word of God speaks of the overcomers that shall prevail.

Rev 12:11 **And they overcame him by the blood of the Lamb, and by the word of their testimony; and they loved not their lives unto the death.**

These are the signs of the overcomer. They are covered by the Blood of the Lamb, their very lives testify to the power of God and they would rather die than to dishonor their God.

Rom 14:8 *For whether we live, we live unto the Lord; and whether we die, we die unto the Lord: whether we live therefore, or die, we are the Lord's.* Php 1:20 *According to my earnest expectation and my hope, that in nothing I shall be ashamed, but that with all boldness, as always, so now also Christ shall be magnified in my body, whether it be by life, or by death. For to me to live is Christ, and to die is gain.*

To be an overcomer we must love God more than we love anything else. There must be nothing in this world that means more to us than God, even life itself. Therein lies the key to overcoming. And so my opinion as to the three categories of what it means to be an over-comer? I reject the commonly held view of #3. I believe it to be an amalgam of 1&2. Jesus is calling those who are living in manner not pleasing to Him. He is reaching out His hand to those who are living in a manner that will lead them to ultimately reject Him. He is calling on all those of Christendom who now dwell in the valley of decision. They must not comfort themselves with the false notion that they will simply "lose rewards." Look again at the right hand column and read it through, then read the left hand column, see if you believe that these people are merely losing rewards. Right now Jesus counsels all those who straddle the world and His Kingdom, before it is too late, to buy from Him *"gold refined in the fire, that you may be rich; and white garments that you may be clothed, that the shame of your nakedness may not be revealed and anoint your eyes with eye salve, that you may see."*

Jesus is forever reaching out His hand. He would have that none would be lost. It is His heart that all would be saved, that all would be overcomers and partake in the promises that He has made to those who are faithful until the end, to those who overcome, to the over-comers. He would have that all would be overcomers. This is how great His love is and even at this late hour He is calling out, He is crying out, with a loud voice and with the same Spirit that said *"O Jerusalem, Jerusalem, thou that killest the prophets, and stonest them which are sent unto thee, how often would I have gathered thy children together, even as a hen gathereth her chickens under her wings, and ye would not!*

Can you hear Him saints? Can you sense the urgency of the hour? Stand fast and do not be moved. Compel those who are wavering to stand fast for our God is coming and He is coming soon. Let us not be overcome by the world but let us overcome the world because we stand upon Him who has already overcome. Stay vigilant and diligently seek Him for He is a rewarder of those that do, the only reward that has any eternal value, His presence. Those who overcome will indeed be rewarded with the only reward worth having; to dwell in His presence for evermore, to lose that would be to lose eternity.

5.

IS GOD IS CALLING HIS REMNANT OUT OF THE ESTABLISHED CHURCH?

"Beware that you do not forget the LORD your God by not keeping His commandments, His judgments, and His statutes which I command you today, lest when you have eaten and are full, and have built beautiful houses and dwell in them; and when your herds and your flocks multiply, and your silver and your gold are multiplied, and all that you have is multiplied; when your heart is lifted up, and you forget the LORD your God who brought you out of the land of Egypt, from the house of bondage; who led you through that great and terrible wilderness, in which were fiery serpents and scorpions and thirsty land where there was no water; who brought water for you out of the flinty rock; who fed you in the wilderness with manna, which your fathers did not know, that He might humble you and that He might test you, to do you good in the end then you say in your heart, "My power and the might of my hand have gained me this wealth." (Deut 8:11-17)

For students of the Bible, the concept of the wilderness should be most familiar. Abraham left his homeland and family to venture forth into an unknown land of promise. Moses left the palatial comforts of Egypt to dwell among the rocks and wild beasts. The tribes of Israel wandered 40 years in the wilderness prior to occupying the land of Canaan. Job lost everything that He might glimpse the Eternal One at the edge of the valley of death. David fled from Saul and spent years eluding him in the pathless wilderness. Most, if not all of the Lord's holy and faithful prophets abandoned all they knew and loved to live alone with the Lord in His company and care. John the Baptist conducted his prophetic ministry as one "crying in the wilderness." Jesus was led by the Holy Spirit into the wilderness forty days and forty nights, tempted of the devil and ministered to by angels. The Apostle Paul spent much of His life and ministry imprisoned, isolated, imperiled and alone. And the woman of Revelations 12 is sheltered and nourished in the wilderness immediately prior to our Lord's return to this earth. My friends, this wilderness theme runs all through the Scriptures, and through the varied lives and experience of God's children. It has always been an essential concept to be grasped, yet I believe this may be more true today. It is vital that we understand what it teaches us about how our Heavenly Father, the Son and the Holy Spirit bring us to true faithfulness and blessing.

Now the concept of the wilderness as it affects others is one thing – yet the actual experience of the wilderness as it impacts our own life and faith is quite another. It is a very intimate matter you see, challenging everything we think we know about God and the Christian life, the church and community, the actual and the superficial. It is wrought with difficult questions and seemingly few answers. It is typically invested with profound emotion, loneliness and even confusion. And it is more of a valley than a mountain-top, with again, seemingly little evidence that heaven is still there, and that Our Lord is still caring for His sheep. To understand the wilderness we must go deeper and further into the very heart and mind of our Heavenly Father, as He loves and nurtures His children. We must look beyond our teachers and books, for they, by and large, don't really understand it. We must divest ourselves of any fluffy religious notions that really don't get to the heart of a man or what really happened in that garden. We must also resist the theological urge to generalize and systematize, as God's wilderness is as varied as His people, and as unlimited as His vast, creative mind.

We are addressing this topic generally, in order that we might understand it better. We are also more specifically hoping to edify and encourage those who like ourselves, find themselves outside and apart from the traditional church organization, having left it behind in order to more perfectly hear and follow the Lord.

The Exodus from the Organized Church

Today we are witnessing an interesting phenomenon where many – God knows the numbers – are leaving the relative structure and security of organized churches, denominations and memberships, to follow hard after their God, to a wilderness of sorts, a strange and unfamiliar place little understood by establishment Christianity. Perhaps the Lord is calling His remnant to Himself in simplicity and purity at the end of this age? Perhaps the prophetic ministry from outside the walls has begun, or at the very least is being perpetuated at this time? Perhaps a time of final testing for the church and Israel is poised to begin? Whatever the ultimate reason, many are coming out, and almost immediately they will need to adapt to this new and strange environment where the Lord alone is all that they have.

It is quite common to hear the following sentiments today from God's people

"The glory of God has left my church."

"Jesus is no longer at the center of our fellowship!"

"My church has aligned itself with the ways of man and the world."

"My church functions more like a club, than an expression of the life of Jesus Christ!"

"The Holy Spirit has gone out of the church."

"The church is of the world and the world is in the church."

Indeed, the world has infiltrated the church to such a degree, and corruption has become so rampant and pervasive that it is practically impossible to keep abreast of all of the apostasy and defilement within. By much spiritual evidence and observation, the 'church on the corner' is either dying or already dead. This is obvious and apparent to any with eyes to see, to those with true spiritual insight. Only those with a vested and carnal interest in perpetuating the corpse, and holding it up with strings will deny this. True spiritual discernment speaks otherwise however. A.W. Tozer and Leonard Ravenhill, for example, 20-40 years back can still be heard on creaky recordings woefully proclaiming the life of God pouring out of contemporary Christianity. Theirs were the prophetic forewarnings from within, all decrying the forces marshaled against the historic church - materialism, humanism, pragmatism, psychology, modern marketing, etc. Then, such corruptive forces were pressing at the edges; today they are rooted into the very fiber of institutional Christianity, across all lines, divisions and denominations. Those who would weep the tears of our Lord are indeed weeping, with great heaviness of spirit and heart.

"Come out of her my people!" is the message of the hour! Come out of her, lest you share in her sins! But to where and to what – this is the question of the hour? Quite often when the Lord draws us out of something and back to Himself, we are led by way of the wilderness. It is this wilderness that concerns us here, and by His grace we will endeavor to more completely comprehend it.

6

WHAT IT IS AND WHY

In this chapter I would like to touch on some key elements in this wilderness experience, including what it is, and why our Lord, in His infinite and loving wisdom might draw His children into such a condition. Perhaps you reading this now are in what you might consider a wilderness, alone with God, cut off in large measure from all you have ever trusted or known. Nothing now seems to make sense, even your religion or relationship with God. Everything appears dark and the way forward seems unfamiliar. Your faith is challenged like never before. The ground beneath your feet is shifting like loose sand. You turn to fellow saints for help and encouragement, but they just don't seem to understand. All they seem to have is an argument or proof text trying to convince you that you are either in sin or rebellion.

My brothers and sisters, we know that you are out there, and that you may be at this moment feeling isolated and alone. It is our hope and prayer that you will be encouraged and edified by the fact that you are not in any manner abandoned by our Good Shepherd, and that you are still very much in His capable and loving care. This wilderness you are in is not a denial of Christ's blessing on your life by any means, but living proof that He loves you more than you can ever know. Indeed, the wilderness – however it is applied to the servants of the Living God – is first and foremost God's idea. It is His wilderness. It is His way back to Himself. He needs to know that there are no circumstances, nor people that will cause you to deny Him.

He needs to know that He alone is your first love. He needs to know that, stripped of all religion and corporate piety, and spiritual machination, you will seek Him alone, for Himself and His glory. He needs to know that you love Him for Him and not just His gifts, and all of the many things church may have restored to you. All of the biblical examples given above can provide us with valuable insight into what the wilderness is, what it looks like (in general terms, as we are also acutely aware that the wilderness experience is manifest differently for each of us as God's children) and what we can expect to find there. To begin, it is a new and strange place – a circumstance or condition that is foreign to all we know. Consider Abraham and Moses leaving the familiarity and security of their home and family and all they have ever known to venture out into a new and strange land. For the most part they are alone in the wilderness. They often don't know exactly where they are being led. There is little to no explanation. God Himself has called them out, drawing them to Himself that they might follow Him in simple faith and trust. He is their way, and they must look to Him in perfect confidence that His guidance and provision will lead only to blessing.

The Lord, in drawing us to Himself often brings us through the wilderness. Here we learn not to trust in ourselves, but in Him alone. He draws us out of wherever we are that we might learn to lean on Him for everything. He is now our way, and our provision. It is a time of total and absolute dependence on Him. He draws us away from all of the props and dependencies, our friends and family, our everyday structures and support mechanisms, that He might be the All that holds us up, and maintains our lives. We must learn to trust God rather than circumstances or people. We must look for the bread that comes from heaven and the water that comes from the rock. We must turn our backs on all we know, even those we love, so that He might know that we love him first and most, that He is enough if everything and everyone else is stripped from us. I have been considering something that A.W. Tozer once said in a sermon, and it was this – "What if all we Christians had was God?" Not His things, nor blessings per say, but only Him. Not a hundred fired up preachers or prophets telling us about Him, but only Him. Alone with Christ, and He asking us "Do you love Me more than these?" as He did to Peter. "Am I enough for you, or are there other things you desire?" My friends, this is essentially what the wilderness is for – to provide our Lord with the answer to this question.

[Have you ever pondered the idea that the modern church - with all of its structure and activity and paraphernalia - is endeavoring to answer questions that God has probably never even asked? Something to think about.]

All of my life I kept looking for Him in other things – people, groups, movements, trends, systems, you name it. Yet in the end He has brought me to Himself, quite part from anything else that may claim or represent Him. This is the wonderful thing about the wilderness – it reduces everything down to bare Boned, spirit touching flesh reality. It clears away all the haze and noise that may be preventing you from seeing and hearing God.

If you have become a Christian, for example, to gain friends and community - if this is what you seek primarily – then the wilderness will isolate you so that He is your only friend and fellowship. Then our Lord will ask you bluntly – Am I enough for you? Do you Love me more than these? If Christianity and church membership is mostly about a healthy environment for yourself and your kids, for activities and programs, then here again, the wilderness will reveal this for the idol it is. The Lord must know, you see. And we must know also, and many will admit that so much of what we do as "church" today keeps us from coming into direct and personal contact with essential things.

The wilderness is a wonderful instrument for stripping away all of our dependencies on things and shadows isn't it? It is about survival and spiritual reality, life and death, hunger and thirst, breathing in and breathing out. Is He your All, my brother? Does living for Him alone define you my sister? We are religious by nature, but only His nature in us, refined and perfected by His Holy Breath and Spirit will satisfy the burning ache in your spirit. We must have Him, and know Him, and want Him, and trust Him, before He will grant to us all of the many blessings pouring out of Him. Is the wilderness a pleasant place? Not really – not how the world measures things anyway – for only here it seems do we come to recognize what we are actually made of, that we are carnal and earthbound, that our faith is largely theoretical, not tried and tested in the fiery furnace of experience. Like earthbound Jacob, wrestling with the Lord, we come to the end of ourselves that He might begin in us anew. Yet we also come to see our God for what He is, in all of His Transcendent Wisdom and Glory; in all of His Grace and Truth, and Love and Light. In seeing Him as He truly is everything else is seen as it really is. Every created thing, including ourselves, can be seen in its true light, the Light of the Bright and Morning Star, the Daystar that scatters all darkness. As there are so few distractions, everything in the wilderness is reduced to the most basic of questions, like -

"Do you love Me more than these" and, "Who is this who darkens counsel By words without knowledge?"

My brethren, I am sorry if this seems so different from what you have been taught to expect. Yet it is the truth and it is the Lord's way. It is not the church's way, and so for the most part those affiliated with it will spurn it, and judge it as illegitimate. Those who seek to save us from all that such a wilderness will present, will obviously fight against it with all they have. It represents no small threat to all organization and mediated leadership; to the self-exalted priest class that has come to rule so much of the body of Christ in our day. Read Job's account and affirm what some of us have already discovered in our wilderness walk – that even God's peace and presence is seemingly withdrawn, causing us to question how much we really trust Him. Even when He withholds the manifest evidence of His presence, when He appears to have turned His back to us and stopped His ears, will we continue to bless Him and to love Him? Despite an often prolonged and overwhelming sense of bewilderment, discouragement, isolation and even guilt, will He remain our only Hope, our Heavenly Father and Loving Shepherd? Will we hold fast to Him or let Him go? Trust is often forged in darkness and silence, when our experience and expectation of what this new life means appears to be in contradiction. My friends – this reveals yet another aspect of God's wilderness.

All of the so-called experts tell us how human beings innately require a community; yet what happens when the Lord is our only community, when all we have is Him, when even the ones we love abandon and forsake us? When all of their words make us feel only guilt and even more bewilderment, when they cannot seem to comprehend the legitimacy of what is happening to us. So much easier to pray down God and all His angels to extricate us from our isolation and hardship. And it is inconceivable to so many believers, not knowing the Lord or His wilderness, that this very thing could be sanctioned and even enabled by God Himself, out of His love and mercy for His beloved children.

"I will build my church", proclaimed the Lord Jesus Christ. Yet this is apparently not good enough for the many man-size church-builders among us, who seek to separate us from God with all their various methods and mediators. By directing all of their resources at maintaining and perpetuating their precious institutions, they fail to recognize that the God they serve doesn't care one bit for their institutions. He cares for His children and will spare no effort – even resorting to the wilderness if necessary – in building them up to perfection in His Beloved Son! Hear this please, all those who have ears to hear. I believe the Lord may be trying to get the attention of His people.

7

THE WILDERNESS; PART OF GOD'S LARGER PLAN

We like to be busy don't we? We almost have an inborn, driving need to advance, to move forward, to do great things for the Lord. Results and numbers and growth are the gilded idols of our day, and they have penetrated the church of Jesus Christ. My friends, if the Lord Himself was so concerned about tangible results and numerical growth, then why did He choose to sideline the greatest evangelist who ever lived? Why indeed did the Apostle Paul spend so much of his ministry shipwrecked, on remote islands, and in prison when the entire world awaited? Have you ever wondered about this? I have. Perhaps the Lord was ministering unto Paul during this wilderness time? Perhaps He didn't want Paul to get too heady about all of the wonderful things (the results) God was doing through Him? Perhaps our Lord was communicating intimately with Paul some of the awesome concepts and revelations found today in His epistles to the churches? Perhaps there were people and connections that could only be cultivated there in the wilderness, off the beaten path, there in the shadows?

My brethren – there really is so much the Lord does not allow us to see, in terms of His larger plan, isn't there? To our carnal nature, and to all that we are as men and even Americans, this wilderness makes absolutely no sense at all. We want to get into the game desperately, and yet the Lord wants us on the sidelines, or maybe even outside the arena and cut off entirely from all the action. He wants us to Himself. He wants to know if He is enough all by Himself, Independent of His gifts and blessings, and all of the noise and trappings of religion and community.

But for how long, you say? Certainly not for years and years? My dear brethren – it is up to Him entirely as our wise and loving Father. Consider that David, running for his life from King Saul in the wilderness, could have ended his isolation on more than one occasion. Yet he trusted in the Lord, that at His appointed time, he would be restored to the fellowship of Israel and his family. Keep this in mind when you are tempted to forsake the wilderness on your own terms.

Consider Job's friends who sought to persuade him to curse God and die. Heaven is silent while the church is having a party down the block. What will you do? You look for sense when nothing, not God, nor the situation itself, makes any sense at all. Explanations are few, if at all. You can either come to hate the wilderness and seek a way out, or you can trust He who loves you enough to allow such things. His plan is so much larger and wider and deeper than our loneliness and disillusionment. As God, He is under no obligation to reveal all or even any aspect of it to us. Is the devil in the wilderness? Likely He is. Yet the Lord and His angels are there too, ministering to us, teaching us, tearing us down and binding us up, comforting and communing with us, revealing His glory to us in quiet revelation and intimate miracles. It is the place where a still small voice can always be heard, where the grandest and god-sized things are reduced down that we might grasp them and go with them. It is the barren and rugged terrain of the prophet not the priest; where created things are laid naked before the great "I Am"- that Awesome, Uncreated One who broods over all the earth, seeking merely one who will prove faithful.

The Wilderness and His Remnant

My friends – I don't pretend to see it all clearly yet, but I believe that in these Last Days the remnant of the Lord (the few out of the many) will commune with Him in the wilderness in preparation for His coming. Always between the gardens is a wilderness, it seems, where saints have long hungered and thirsted after God. Perhaps it is in the wilderness where the Church and Israel are ultimately reconciled in the heart of God? The Book of Revelation hints at this. Perhaps in these last tumultuous days, there is spiritual and even physical protection to be found here for the Lord's own? Perhaps the true church of Jesus Christ has always been a wilderness people, largely unreported, off the radar, disenfranchised, de-legitimized by establishment and institutional Christianity? Quietly and faithfully and simply, they go on serving the Lord in the back alleys of life, away from the rush and clamor of church bells and choirs? Is your faith rugged enough, my brother? Has it been tested by wind and storm, my sister? Can you still follow Him without a scripted program, a schedule, a holy day, a church bulletin? Can you worship Him without a music director, without a big band and choir, without the predictable lyric of the song sheet?

He is coming! And He will first come to His own. If this be true, and it is - then where will they be found in these final hours of Adam's reign? What will be sustaining them as they wait patiently for Him – will it be the bread from heaven and the water from the rock? Or will it be the delicacies of Egypt – meat and wine that turns foul in their bellies? When all mediators between them and God are removed, and He stands before them, will they be able to recognize Him, and love Him, and hear Him? Will His sheep-follow Him at this time when their very lives will depend on it?

8

THE SPIRIT OF GIDEON

Now in the days of Gideon, a time of judgment, the Midianites and the Amikalites oppressed the children of God. No matter what the Israelites planted, they never got to see the fruits of their labor. The Midianites and the Amakilites would come in like locusts and devour everything. And so, Israel was greatly impoverished. Can I suggest that we face the same landscape and problems in Christendom today? We are impoverished spiritually and financially and no matter the work done, it is consumed by the idols and the enemy which seems to be all around us like locusts.

Now, in their distress, the children of Israel cried out to God for a deliverer, and the Lord sent them a prophet. The prophet reminded them of God's faithfulness and how they had rejected Him (Jud 6:8-10) Now, at God's appointed time, when all is desolate, He speaks to Gideon who was threshing wheat in the winePress in an effort to hide his activities from their oppressors.(6-11) *The Lord is with you mighty man of valor.*" You see how God is calling what is not as it would be. Hiding from your enemies in a defunct winepress in an effort to get some bread is hardly the stuff of valor. Brothers and sisters, I want you to see Gideon as a type of the Remnant God is in the process of raising up right now. Do not focus on the 300 as of yet, for that is still a ways off. We as people are not ready yet. Listen to what Gideon says to the Lord.

"Oh my Lord, if the Lord is with us, then why has all this happened to us? And where are all the miracles which our Fathers told us about saying,

'Did not the Lord bring us up from Egypt?" But now the Lord has forsaken us and delivered us into the hands of the Midianites."(v 13)

How many of us today, brothers and sisters, would cry out the same thing as Gideon just did? Does it not seem to you that we are surrounded by darkness on every side? Maybe in your personal life you feel forsaken? Maybe it's been a long time since you have experienced the presence of God if ever? Have you ever said in your own heart, just like Gideon "Where are all the miracles?" Maybe it's been a long time since you have seen a loved one or anyone for that matter, well saved and radically regenerated?

And after Gideon gets through with his complaints to God, the Lord speaks to him and says *"Go in the might of yours and you shall save Israel.........have I not sent you?"* (v 14) You see how God refuses to take on board what Gideon has just complained about and again affirms His calling on Gideon's life? Saints, take heart at this for God has called you, listen to how Gideon replies and see if this reflects your own heart. " How can I save Israel? *Indeed my clan is the weakest in Manasseh and I am the least in my father's house."* (v15) To which the Lord replies *"Surely I will be with you."*

Can you see how the Lord picked the weakest man from the weakest clan? It's not about the man brothers and sisters, it's about the God that goes with the man. If God is with us, who can be against us? This truly represents the Remnant believers today. We are the weakest men and women. The reply that Gideon gave to God is the right reply in the right spirit. Without God we are nothing and can do nothing, but by the same token, when God is with us, and He says to Gideon *"Surely I will be with you,"* then there is nothing we cannot do. This is the spirit of the people of God today. They acknowledge their own weakness and this is through their personal experience. They have experienced failure and they know what it is like to feel abandoned, this has been a journey and it ends with them knowing their utter helplessness without God being with them

Now brothers and sisters, this is a theme all through Scriptures. Consider what Moses says after forty years in the desert after fleeing Egypt and believing (rightly) that he would be used to deliver his people. Again it comes in encounter and the Lord commissioning, this time in a burning bush *"Who am I that I should bring the children of God out of Israel?* (Ex 3:11) You see, as with Gideon, there is an encounter with God. Consider Jeremiah as he encounters God" Before I formed you in the womb I knew you. Before you were born I sanctified you. I ordained you as a prophet to the nations. Then said I, Ah Lord behold I cannot speak for I am a youth." (Jer 1:6) You see the reluctance of the prophets who know their limitations but it is God who calls and it is God who sends and it is God who goes before.

One more example would be the prophet Isaiah in chapter six. He encounters God and cries out *"Woe is me for I am undone because I am a man of unclean lips."* (Isa 6:5) There are many objections, and they are sound reasons, these prophets are not lying when they tell God how unworthy they are or how unable they are or how they cannot speak or are so very very weak. God knows these things. Yet God will share His Glory with no man. He picks the weak things of this world to confound the wise and to bring glory to Himself. It is He who does the calling, and it is obedience to the calling that is required. If you are not allowing God to use you because of how weak you are then maybe all of these prophets should not have moved forward with God either?

The Lord raises up who He will. And now, in these latter days, He and He alone is raising up a remnant. And despite all of your objections, it matters not for He deliberately raises up the weak and the overlooked so that the glory that is soon to cover the earth as the waters cover the sea will be all His. He is raising up the broken and the battered, the lowly and the humble, to come against the proud and the strong and the mighty and the many.

After Gideon's encounter with God he begs Him not to leave. (v18) Can I tell you saints, one encounter with God, with the presence of God, ruins you for this life. His presence will become your all-consuming passion. Gideon, in a day of poverty and famine, insists on sacrificing to the Lord and he prepares the little that he had and he offers it to God. This is what happens saints when we encounter the living God. What was ours becomes His. We gladly give Him what we have, and if it is only a widow's mite, we see from Scripture that the Lord is well pleased with this kind of sacrifice. Gideon's sacrifice to God was well pleasing and acceptable, we see this because fire falls on acceptable sacrifice and consumes it. What will you sacrifice saints?

After the offering Gideon cries out *"I have seen the angel of the Lord face to face."* (v22) This changes Gideon forever. Saints, have you had such an encounter? Has your life been drastically changed from the inside out? This encounter, not unlike Isaiah, was so traumatic that God has to speak into Gideon and say *"Peace be with you, do not fear, you shall not die."* (v23) Now, how can we tell if we ourselves have been effected as Gideon? Well, when one encounters the Lord then idols have to go. Nothing can come between God and His people. And this is exactly what Gideon is called to do. The children of Israel in that day worshiped Baal just as those that surrounded them did. There will be a severe price to pay if Gideon breaks down the altar of Baal, in fact, it means almost certain death. I wonder what we would do today if the Lord challenged us in the same way He challenged Gideon. What idols of today might the Lord require to be torn down?

Gideon gets himself ten others who are willing to go with him, and at night, they tear down the altar of Baal. It does not take the people long to figure out who tore down their idol's altar. They find Gideon's father and demand that he hand over Gideon to be killed. Now, in wisdom that undoubtedly came from God, Gideon's father says to the crowds that if Baal is so all-powerful, why are they here pleading on his behalf? Surely Baal is strong enough to exact revenge on his own? This argument works and of course Gideon did not die for Baal is a false God. Now, every time the people saw Gideon it was a testimony to the impotency of the god that they worshipped. Can you say, brothers and sisters, that you are a living testimony to the impotency of the enemy of our soul?

Saints, God is raising up a remnant people who are a testimony to the one true living God. By defying the convention and idols and gods of our day, then we ourselves become a testimony and a witness to the world. Can you see the process we have to go through prior to the ultimate defeat of our adversary? God's children have to follow the same path as Gideon, before ever being involved in mightier battles to come. First Gideon had to see the desolation of a country devoid of God. Then he had to believe that he had been forsaken because this truly highlights our utter helplessness outside of God. Then he had to encounter God and see himself as he truly was, so that when God accomplishes great things through him he will be in no doubt that it was not by might nor power but by God's Spirit and the Spirit alone. Then we see the hunger and thirst after Gideon's encounter with the Lord and his willingness to give all that he had. It's in this process that it is learned that God has called us, He prepares us and He anoints us. Then there is the obedience to defy the culture of the day and live as God has called us to live.

This is the preparation process. There can be no shortcuts. Where are you in this process saints? Be encouraged, know that you have been called and you will be sent. Remember that God used the weakest man from the weakest clan who complained of being forsaken. Do not say that God cannot use you, for it is by calling that you are called. Follow the example of Gideon and continue to prepare. The time is short saints, the remnant are being raised. Reject the world and all that it has to offer and rise with them by the hand of God.

9.

D-DAY APPROACHES.

And Jesus went forth, and saw a great multitude, and was moved with compassion toward them, and he healed their sick. And when it was evening, his disciples came to him, saying, This is a desert place, and the time is now past; send the multitude away, that they may go into the villages, and buy themselves victuals. But Jesus said unto them, they need not depart; give ye them to eat. And they say unto him, we have here but five loaves, and two fishes. He said, bring them hither to me. (Mat 14:14-18)

There is a great multitude today who are desperately hungry and thirsty. All over the world the people dwell in great darkness and the darkness increases every day. Hell has opened its vaults and is beginning to spew out evil with increasing speed and urgency because it knows its time is short. There is desperate darkness coming and it is coming at us with alarming speed. Yet, as in the time of Noah, the world is ignorant of the impending disaster about to befall it. Like the children of Israel when Jesus says "O Jerusalem, Jerusalem, the one killing the prophets and stoning those who are sent to her, how often would I have gathered your children together, even as a hen gathers her chicks under her wings, and you would not!"

Jesus wept because He knew that less than forty years after His death and resurrection that the whole system would come tumbling down. The Temple would be destroyed and the Israelites would be no more as a nation and they had absolutely no idea. In those days, it was unimaginable that their Temple, their country, their way of life would be swept away and that they would be scattered to the four corners of the earth. Can you imagine our Democratic system being washed away? Can you imagine the fall of America? Why is that thought any harder to comprehend? Can you imagine the Church system being swept away?

In 1940, the British Expeditionary Force (BEF) found itself routed. It had been sent to Europe to aid the French and the Belgians against the might of the German army. Yet, the strongest army in the world failed. The Germans pursued them and only a gallant rear guard action allowed most of the British to escape and head toward the coast in a full retreat. They congregated at a town called Dunkirk. In that small port town, there were over 400,000 allied troops, British, French and Belgians. Disaster was staring Britain in the face. What was about to unfold was nothing less than the destruction of the bulk of the British forces and conditional surrender to the Germans was discussed by the politicians back in Britain. In an act of desperation, Churchill called for a national day of prayer. All over Britain the church bells rang out and Christians cried out to God in prayer to save the men.

Inexplicably, Hitler stopped his forces from advancing, this lasted three days. Historians to this day have no idea why he stopped. One theory was that it was at the advice of his astrologer. Another was that the Luftwaffe and the Vermacht argued over who would have the glory of finishing of the might of the British army, one more theory was that Hitler hoped to negotiate with, and neutralize the British. What we do know was that he stopped his advance long enough for the Brits to initiate "Operation Dynamo." Now you Greek scholars out there know that the Greek word for power is dynamus. It is ironic to me that the operation would be named this. Here we have the mightiest force the world has ever seen, the British navy. It was to be sent over to attempt to rescue as many men as they could from the beaches.

They knew they faced an almost impossible task and even by their own estimations, they believed that they may have only been able to save 20 to 50,000. Their greatest fear was that they would be bombed in the harbor and have ships sunk thus rendering the harbor useless. After three days Hitler ordered his troops on the move again. And so, with great desperation "Operation Dynamo" swung into action. And every day that passed, the Germans came closer and closer and every day the Luftwaffe bombed the soldiers on the beaches and the British navy mercilessly. And of course, the greatest fear of the British came to pass. Boats sunk in the harbor rendered the harbor useless. Now all seemed lost.

In one last ditch desperate effort, a call was sent out to everyone near the English Channel in Britain who had a small boat. (Infamously treacherous waters, 22 miles wide) to cross over and save whoever they could. And so, an armada of small boats, fishing boats, pleasure boats, tug boats, pulling behind rowing boats began to cross the waters. The waters were reported to be strangely calm. Incredibly, in the next several days, they managed to take 340,000 men off the beach. Where the might of the British army had failed, where the strongest force the world have ever known, the British navy failed, God used an armada of "little ships" to save the western world from complete destruction. You have to remember that it was from Britain that "D Day" was launched. If the Brit's had been destroyed at that time, most of the Western world would have forever fallen under the shadow and the jack-boot of some of the most evil men the world has ever known.

Now brothers and sisters, I want you to think of this true story as an analogy. This great evil that is engulfing our world in these final days are like the Germans bearing down on those hundreds and thousands of soldiers. The soldiers are the multitude. The British Navy is the Established church. The small ships are the Remnant. The British Navy were shown to be powerless. The Established church is just as powerless. The end is fast approaching and we are looking at a Church that has proven itself to be powerless. They are powerless to reach the lost, powerless to stand effectively in this day of evil. It is a church without the power and the presence of God. What moved the hand of God in this story? It was the prayers of the saints. Who did God use to rescue the soldiers on the beaches? He used the "Little ships." And the little ships may well ask in this present day "who are we that God could use us?" God will use His Remnant people. God's Remnant people are like those little ships. Willing to go and face what seemed like certain death in order to rescue the 'multitude.' The Lord took five loaves and two fish and fed a multitude. He took a tiny amount of food in His hand and He broke it and He fed it to the multitude. God will take a small amount of people, break them, and use them to feed the hungry souls and to give water to the thirsty. Has the Lord broken you? Have you yielded to the hand of God? God is raising up a small army, a small armada of "small ships,' broken yielded vessels to do His work and He will receive all the honor and the glory.

If you have been broken, if you "love not your souls unto death," then it is time to cast yourselves into the waters of life. There is a multitude out there desperate and dying. Their future is certain without the help of the little ships. There is a force of darkness bearing down on the world right now and it will sweep away the world as we know it. Only the broken of the Lord will be a power on the earth. Only the Remnant of God's people will be a light in the darkness. Now is the time brothers and sisters. Lift up your heads, our salvation draws nigh.

10.

HELL SHAKING LOVE.

I am not of the pre-trib rapture position. And that is the last you will hear me mention any such phrases because I believe if we use certain phrases then we simply get pigeon- holed. Enough to say that I would soundly reject the very premise of the "Left behind" series. We will go through the great tribulation and we will suffer and most of us who are alive at that time will be martyred.

Now, the many positions that Christians take on last days are well documented. I would encourage everyone to read the Scriptures and allow the Holy Spirit to lead and guide you into the truth. Do not follow men and the teachings of men on these matters. You must be convinced in your spirit of these things that are shortly to come to pass. Now, as one who went to Bible school and who aced his "premillennial dispensationalism" class (should have got the A just for being able to say and spell it) I could certainly give you the historical views of the three main positions and would also be able to tell you about the birth of dispensationalism and the pre-trib-rapture theory. But, I am not going to do that. You can certainly do the research yourself and come to your own conclusions. As I said, ultimately the Holy Spirit has to teach you and lead you and guide you. I am just going to share with you my burden and what I believe is shortly to come to pass. You of course, are free to agree or to disagree or take what you will and leave the rest.

I believe that persecution is coming to the Church, the Remnant, whoever truly belongs to Jesus. I do not believe that God's hand will be stayed in this because I believe that He has His purpose and it is part of the prophetic calendar. So let me lay out for you how I "see" the times that are approaching. There is something that we call Christendom. To me, that is everything that calls itself by the name of Christ. This would include every denomination, including Catholics, Pentecostals, Baptists, Evangelicals a host of Non-denominational churches and the man in the street who does not go to any church but if you were to push him, he would call himself either a believer or a Christian.

Now let me say plainly, I believe that only a very small percentage of that which calls itself Christian is in fact true born-again, new creature in Christ, sold out disciples of Jesus. Various men have given numbers over the years, Ravenhill once said that he reckoned only 7% of professing Christians in America were actually Christians. The truth is, I have no idea. I do know that Jesus said that many were called but few were chosen and that the road to heaven was a narrow one and few there were that found it. That's not so complicated and I see no need to complicate it further by adding to what Jesus said.

And so how will the persecution come about and who will persecute the saints of God, martyring them and believing they are doing God a favor by doing it? Well, I believe that the vast majority of Christendom that is not saved will soon morph into the great whore church. What is this great whore church? Well it will be a church that will bring together the major religions of the world under one roof. Islam, Judaism and Christianity will join together under a false prophet who will testify to the authenticity of the man of peace, the anti-Christ. Tumultuous circumstances in the world will give rise to this anti-Christ. People of every nation will be mesmerized by him and by his displays of power. Only the saints will not fall for this grand delusion. And as they refuse to follow him they become the targets of hatred of the world in general and specifically the religious.

Now I believe that there will be a direct correlation between the rise of persecution and the pouring out of God's Spirit upon His people. What will come first I do not know. I lean towards persecution coming first and God pouring His Spirit into His people in order for them to deal with this, yet I also believe that prior to the beginnings of the great tribulation that God will pour out His Spirit upon His people in measure and that this will really be the beginnings of a deep hatred from the religious people. You see, there are many who desire to see a great outpouring of His Spirit but there are few who embrace the cross of Calvary, few who embrace the hard narrow path of the Word of God.

And so who amongst us can embrace a God that has martyrdom in mind for us? Some may see this kind of thinking as some kind of doom and gloom preaching. Yet, the people who I am writing this for know very well that this is not so. You see, the Bride-groom is coming back for His bride the Church. We know that the time is short. And so we would celebrate the end of the ages because the Lord is coming. We know that we have been walking through a dry and thirsty land, a land in the midst of famine, and whatever it takes for God to pour out His Spirit in power, then the child of God embraces that. If it takes a mighty confrontation on the mountain for the rain to come, then so it must be. If the word has to go out "choose ye this day whom you will serve," then that word must go out. If the five virgins without oil must be warned then they must be warned. If there is a generation of saints that are alive at the culmination of the ages and that generation has to be us, then praise the Lord for He knows what He is doing.

Saints, we know that we do not battle against flesh and blood but against principalities and powers. When those principalities and powers know that their time is short, what would we expect from such great darkness? If God increases the light in His children, if He pours out His Spirit as in the latter rains, what would we expect the enemy of our souls to do? Sit idly by? No, we know that there is a time coming such as has never been before. The time is coming when every child of God will be hunted down and killed by the anti-Christ. Yet I want you to know that this scenario also includes the filling of saints in such a fashion that they could not even imagine. The power that we will have will be the power to resist the greatest evil that the world has ever seen. We will be filled with a hell-shaking love, the same hell destroying love that we witnessed on Calvary. The same hell shaking love that we saw in our brother Stephen as he was stoned to death.

If you have ever experienced the presence of God, the manifest presence of God then the scenario of being filled with such perfect love that casts out all fear is one that is to be relished. To walk in the power of our Lord, to walk in the Spirit in such a fashion that has yet to be witnessed on the earth, this is a glorious prospect for God's children. The genuine saint has spent all of his walk with the Lord with an earnest desire to be more like Him. Genuine persecution and refining fire only kills the flesh in us, it does nothing to the Spirit of God in us. And so the more the genuine saint is persecuted, the more of Christ the world will see. As the world comes against us with all of the fury of hell behind it, it will only see a greater expression of Jesus. This is the paradox, the irony, the ultimate weakness of evil, the ultimate triumph of good over evil.

Now brothers and sisters, are we that people? Can you say that the desire of your life is to be more like Jesus and to follow Him? Do you love Him above all else? Are you worthy to be His disciple? Now is the time to have your Gethsemane. The battle of Calvary was won in the garden of Gethsemane. Will you turn back when these things begin to unfold? And so the question bears repeating "Who amongst us can embrace a God that has called us to martyrdom?" Remember, when it became clear that the Lord Jesus was to become a suffering servant, one who was to be despised by the multitude, rejected, humiliated, tortured and then crucified, how many stood with Him? If you have to face the same things in the coming persecution, will you still stand with Him? Jesus urged His disciples to pray because He knew what was about to come to pass, He Himself prayed and overcame the flesh in the garden before the time came and He found victory in the Garden. He had made up His mind that He would bow to the will of His Father. Can you do the same saint? Can you make up your mind now that come what may, if events of the end time are not how you supposed them to be or have been taught that they will be, that nevertheless you will bow to the will of your Father and embrace the God that calls you to martyrdom?

11.

SHEEP FROM GOATS.

There is a separation going on I believe. I believe that the Lord is using hunger and thirst to separate His people. This is why I believe there is a famine going on, a drought across the land. What had been taken for granted years ago has been withdrawn. The void has been filled with soulish activity. The problem with soulish activity is that it can never satisfy, never sustain.

What will truly separate God's people from this world? What will it take? I am not quite sure, but I know that God is coming down. There are five virgins and they have oil in their lamps. Why are the lamps not trimmed? Where is the light? For anyone who has experienced the presence of God, nothing else is acceptable. It's not good enough to stand outside the door, it's not good enough to remain in the courtyard, one must enter in. And the only way to enter in is to pass the altar, the brazen alter. What will we bring as a sacrifice" How will we humble ourselves? What state are we in? Are we able to look at ourselves?

We expect to see the power of God without the sacrifice. We expect that God will come down and legitimize our ministries, He will not. God will come down for His glory and for the love of His people. He will hear their cries, He will see their afflictions, He will see a people ready to glorify Him for no other purpose than to glorify Him. He will not honor nor will he send fire to those who seek to honor themselves. Why do we see no miracles in the church? Why are there no signs and wonders that follow?

We make excuses here in the West that the people are too rational, they are not dependent upon God, their need is not great, they have doctors and so on. All of that may be true, yet God will not honor men's ministries. He will honor the worship of His people. He is not conjured up by louder music or drum beat. No one stands in the presence of God, all are silent before His majesty, all are hushed and awe descends like a blanket upon the heads of His people and their heads are bowed and their hands raised up and trembling. Not because they were instructed to bow their heads, raise their hands, sit, stand, jump.No, no, not in the presence of God. One assumes a position before the living and the mighty God just as a natural instinct. No instructions are required as one is prostrate in His holiness. Every part of who you are is penetrated by light. It is glorious and traumatic all at the same time.

And the oil that dwells within your chest is set aflame by this light, this fire from the throne itself. "Did not our hearts burn within us as we walked with Him?" Yet we are not walking now, we are in the throne room itself, God has come down. Our whole body burns with a beautiful warmth. All things are possible, eternity stretches out before us and we never want to leave this place, we never want to leave this place. The candlestick burns. God speaks, sin melts like wax, refining, yes refining. We offer ourselves and the dross that lies within and the Lord says "Come."

So what will bring this presence down? An awareness of the times and death to business as usual. A genuine desire for God. A return to the biblical example of church. What we have today bears no resemblance whatsoever to what God initiated. We have man centered churches and programs of men. None are bad in and of themselves, they are just not God ordained. They are, for the most part, religious social clubs. I believe that shortly God's people will come out of these social clubs. Madam Guyon writes

I am deeply grieved that so many in this day (she lived 300 years ago, people never change) even some good people, allow themselves to be led astray by the enemy. Has not God warned us against false prophets and lying wonders of the last days? All true prophets have spoken in the name of the Lord- "Thus says the Lord." The enemy gains great advantage because people love

*extraordinary manifestations, signs and wonders. I believe the
inordinate love of external signs is used of the enemy to draw
people away from the Word of God and from the inward way of
faith. The signs that come from God encourage you to die to
yourself.* (Intimacy with Christ..p21)

Madam Guyon spoke prophetically when she said that "the
inordinate love of external signs is used of the enemy to draw
people away from the word of God." According to Barna , this
generation is the most Biblically illiterate generation for almost
300 years.

You see, in 1st Corinthians, the Jews wanted a sign from Jesus that
His power would establish power and dominion over all their
enemies. The Greeks were looking for some brilliant philosophy
that only the very rich and educated could understand, something
that would conquer and better other philosophies of the day
through the sheer power of intellect and man's genius. What they
both got, was Calvary. And by being focused on outward signs and
philosophies, they missed the greatest event in the history of the
planet.

God Himself had stepped into time and space. Not as a rich man,
not a highly educated man, but as a poor working man. The Lord
Jesus was born amongst the filth and stench of a manger, not in a
palace, not in a temple, but in the very lowest reaches of the earth.
If you are a religious man, or a worldly man, Jesus is going to
disappoint you every time. He will not perform at the whim of
men, He came to die. To the Jews a stumbling block, to the
Greeks, foolishness. Let no one doubt though, that Jesus had come
to conquer, and conquer He did. He conquered doubts, He
conquered fears, He conquered death He conquered pride and He
conquered sin.

Yet, in many ways, Calvary is not enough for people. They want,
no demand, victory over their circumstances, a change in
circumstances, anything less is unacceptable. Yet the way of the
cross is the same today as it was then. It signifies death and

victory, not for changed circumstances, but in the very midst of them. We see in the cross, the perfect example of obedience, even although Gethsemane showed the struggle. When we accept the circumstances of our lives, no, embrace them, then we see the miracle. When we surrender to the Lord in the very midst of the most difficult circumstances, laying our lives down, then a whole other world opens up before us, this is the true road of faith.

Sometimes circumstances were overcome by the Apostles, just as many times they were not. Yet the Apostles discovered true faith in the very midst of their trials and tribulations. The Apostle Paul learned to be content in whatever circumstances he found himself in. It is worth remembering that all of the Apostles and a good many of the early church were eventually tortured and killed, were they abandoned by God? Of course not.

Regardless of your circumstances this day, know that Jesus is in the midst of the storm with you. He will take you all the way through if you keep your eyes upon Him and that He calls on us to give thanks in everything. Remember when the Apostles were scourged for Him? They rejoiced. The Holy Spirit tells us to count it all Joy when you fall into various trials for this tests your faith that produces patience. When we face something horrific and life threatening, then we discover why we serve God. Is He our "Genie in a lamp?" or is He our Lord and Master to whom we have sworn to follow, all the way to the cross and beyond.

Now when he was in Jerusalem at the Passover, in the feast day, many believed in his name, when they saw the miracles which he did. But Jesus did not commit himself unto them, because he knew all men, (Joh 2:23-24)

Why would Jesus not commit Himself to these particular followers? Were they not "believers" and had they not seen miracles? What was it about these people that Jesus knew? Listen to what Mathew Henry says about these believers………

They were tumultuous, and wanted discretion and management. These in Jerusalem perhaps had their expectations of the temporal reign of the Messiah more raised than others, and, in that expectation, would be ready to give some bold strokes at the government if Christ would have committed himself to them and put himself at the head of them; but he would not, for his kingdom is not of this world. We should be shy of turbulent unquiet people, as our Master here was, though they profess to believe in Christ, as these did., knew the wickedness of some and the weakness of others. The evangelist takes this occasion to assert Christ's omniscience. 1. He knew all men, not only their names and faces, as it is possible for us to know many, but their nature, dispositions, affections, designs, as we do not know any man, scarcely ourselves. He knows all men, for his powerful hand made them all, his piercing eye sees them all, sees into them. He knows his subtle enemies, and all their secret projects; his false friends, and their true characters; what they really are, whatever they pretend to be. He knows them that are truly his. IV. That the reason why he did not commit himself to them was because he knew them

But he answered and said unto them, an evil and adulterous generation seeketh after a sign; and there shall no sign be given to it, but the sign of the prophet Jonas: (Mat 12:39)

The Lord will not commit to those who are not committed to Him. This present generation of loud and "tumultuous" believers are seeking to establish the Lords kingdom here on earth. The sign the Lord gave them is not good enough for them. What sign did the Lord give them? He gave them the sign of the Prophet Jonah. When all aboard the ship knew that they were lost, Jonah was sacrificed to save them. He then spent 3 days in the belly of the whale. All of mankind was and is caught up in a great storm of darkness and tumult. It is to Calvary that one must look. In the quiet of faith the Lord will respond to His own, He always has and He always will, but He will not respond to a crass church which seeks to gratify their own corrupt lusts. So all of the churches that cry out for miracles, the Lord knows the motivations of their heart. Signs and wonders would follow. Follow what? The preaching of Calvary. The proclamation of the Truth. The bold witness for Christ. The unashamed stance of the one truly committed. The genuine love of the lost, expressed in practical terms. So, those who place the cart before the horse do so for a reason. And in doing so, they expose the fragile nature of the faith that they claim to have.

The Lord will not commit to those who have built their houses on sinking sand. This is why we see the "house," of "believers," come tumbling down when faced with "unanswered prayers." For they are not established on the solid Rock of **Jesus** Christ and the cross of Calvary. "On Christ the solid rock I stand, all other ground is sinking sand." Does your faith depend upon you seeing a miracle? Or does your faith stand upon the finished work of the cross of Calvary?

So, who are today's "John 2" believers? Who is it today that the Lord will not commit too? Who today run after signs and wonders? How many churches today, have as their main focus, signs and wonders? Show me a church whose main focus is on signs and wonders, and I will show you a church that neglects the central tenet of Christianity, Jesus Christ and Him crucified. Show me a church whose main focus is on signs and wonders and I will show you a church where the majority reject "dying to self." Show me a church whose main focus is on signs and wonders and I will show you a church with pseudo fellowship. The sinking sand of the modern Pentecostal church is their inordinate love of external signs. This love of extraordinary manifestations, is a compensation for a lack of a true faith which would lead to the death of self. The end results of those who follow this path is a life of self-indulgence, an inability to adhere to sound doctrine, no change in their lives, and no fruit of the Holy Spirit.

And so the few converts that they may see are converts after their own likeness, after their own shallowness. Tozer says that anemic Christians produce anemic converts. Bloodless Christians producing bloodless converts. Only by returning to the foot of the cross can the church find its way back to God. This evil and adulterous generation, that is without Lordship, needs to come to the cross of Christ and commit themselves to death. Only by adhering to this sign, the sign of Jonah, can Christendom hope to see **a reformation** of its powerless state. Christendom today is caught in a great storm, and it is sinking. There is much noise as it thrashes in the heavy seas. As it begins to sink, tossed from a boat carrying them in the wrong direction, they suddenly have found themselves enveloped in a great darkness that is devoid of light. Will they die in the belly of the whale?

12.

TIME FOR A U-TURN?

I believe with all my heart that God's remnant children are being raised up all over the world. They are being separated, like the sheep from the goats, the wheat from the tares. Many of them are in a sort of desert, not of their own choosing, but by the calling of God. In that desert they are learning to depend upon Him entirely so that when the time comes, persecution and so on, that even if none go with them, still they shall follow. Yet that does not change the fact that they have a sincere and genuine desire to have genuine fellowship with those of like-mind, meaning those who burn with a passion for the Lord and are hungry and thirsty for His presence and simply just cannot do business as usual anymore. This is the process of God calling His own. This is the process of counting the cost. Certainly, when the Lord was crucified, one would have to be found outside the walls in order to be identified with Him. To be outside the walls, to be detached from the system is not an easy or a simple thing, it comes with great cost and indeed if it did not it would not be the decision that it is. This calling is only going to get more intense as we move forward, as the day of the Lord approaches. Yet the Lord has called us to gather together, and all the more as we see that day approach and that is why I believe you will begin and are beginning to see a visible representation of these called out children.

I have a GPS system in my car. It's awesome. As a directionally challenged Real Estate agent it has been such a blessing to me. I simply put in the address and follow the blue line and I inevitably end up at my destination. Yet even with this system, you can take wrong turns and the system will automatically "recalculate" and give you new directions to get you back on track. This almost always involves "taking the next exit" or doing a "legal U-turn when possible." Sometimes when you take the wrong road, but it runs near to or initially parallel with the correct road, the system still believes you to be on the right road. As the wrong road slowly veers away from the correct road, the system finally figures it out and re-directs you. Much of Christendom has taken the wrong road. Initially it runs almost parallel to the correct road and without discernment, it is almost impossible to know that you are on the wrong path. Most will simply plow ahead down the road directed and it's at a point of getting lost that the person realizes that they have gone astray. When Amelia Earheart attempted her epic flight, it is reckoned that she only had to be a tiny fraction off in her calculations to miss the Island that she was aiming for by hundreds of miles. To continue flying and being slightly of course, would take her ever further away from her destination. Today, Christendom is moving further and further away from its destination. When the destination ceases to be God Himself, and the destination becomes something other than His presence, His Tabernacle, His alter, His throne room, then we simply get further and further away from Him and the narrow path that leads to Him. Only by getting off at the "next exit," or doing a "legal U-turn," can we get back on the narrow path. The address, the direction itself must always be God Himself. Are you headed in that direction, is that what is plugged into your spirit, is He your destination?

A long time ago the "Church" was redefined by men as something separate from the simple gathering of the saints. They created a building and a system and they called it their own. This is always the folly of men. Consider this, consider what men would do with this. Say we had in our possession, the bush that burned and the sand that surrounded it when Moses encountered the Lord. It would be venerated and visited by the masses of people and it would be worshiped. Yet all it would be would be a bush and some sand. It is the presence of God that makes the ground Holy, whether it is a bush, some sand, a building, a living room, a basement. God dwells within His people. They are the Church. They are living stones, built upon the chief stone, the cornerstone. When two or three of them gather together, then He is there in the midst of them. Two or three brothers and sisters. Not one, for one can worship and pray alone and come before the throne, but to the two or three there lies the promise.

This corporate presence of God is unique and beautiful and Holy and majestic. It cannot be compared. It cannot because it was created that way, praise the Lord. Now if I know that and you know that then the enemy of our souls knows that too. This, I would charge, would become one of his greatest tasks, to destroy genuine gatherings of the saints. He has had much success but has ultimately failed. Just when he thinks he has down a wonderful job, then God begins to call all His children all over the world, His remnant children to come together for these, the final days. What seems like the enemy's greatest victory will become his ultimate defeat. As the saints begin to gather in defiance of his works, then he will reveal himself and come against them with hell and all of its fury. And then, in the midst of all of that, the Bridegroom returns for His bride. The lion of Judah returns and He rides, not on a donkey but on a stallion. Not now as the Lamb but as the Lion. He comes to bring justice and judgement. There will be a fire in His eyes and a two-edged sword in His mouth, glory to God, glory to God.

The Lord says "Look to me, I am the author and the finisher of your faith." Shall we begin in the Spirit and attempt to finish this journey in the flesh? Brothers and sisters, if you would join this ancient army, this kingdom that was and is and is to come, if you would march in lockstep with Gideon and with David and with Joshua, if you would run towards Goliath, if you would take on ten thousand and slay them all, if you would kneel down in the arena of life as the lions approach, if you would take your place with the heroes of faith then it is high time that we take our eyes of ourselves and look up, look up to the cross of Calvary. Brothers and sisters, when I look up I see humility. I see my Lord humbled and naked for the whole world to see. Nothing hidden. When I look up I see justice. I see sin condemned. Oh brothers and sisters when I look up I see mercy, mercy for me, mercy for me, mercy for me. I do not see my own condemnation, I see my Jesus. Yes, I see Jesus. There is therefore, now no condemnation to those who are in Christ Jesus, who walk not according to the flesh, but according to the Spirit. For the law of the Spirit of life in Christ Jesus has made me free from the law of sin and death. Oh what a glorious freedom. Free indeed, free indeed, free indeed. Free indeed to stand and fight. To battle even unto death, with my fellow freed men. I pray today that those whom the Son has set free will push the doors of their captivity of wretchedness, that they would realize their freedom, that they would reckon their freedom and walk out of their cells into the glorious sunlight of no condemnation and join the Lord's army in these the final days of the battle, one more battle in the war that is already won.

Right now, Christendom is in a similar situation to those Israelites of Ezra'a period. We have joined ourselves to the world, and we have lost our distinctiveness. It is no surprise that the world cannot tell us apart from them. In 9:12 The Holy Spirit speaks prophetically through the priest and says "Now therefore, do not give your daughters as wives for their sons, nor take their daughters to your sons, and never seek their peace or prosperity, that you may be strong and eat the good of the land and leave it as an inheritance to your children forever." We, as the church here on earth have given our children, sons and daughters in marriage to the world. We have sought peace by giving up our principles and turning from the word of God. We have sought prosperity and the things of the world and we are not strong. We are entering into the days of the Lords indignation. God says to us in Ezekiel 22:24-25 "You are a land that is not cleansed or rained on in the day of indignation. The conspiracy of her prophets in her midst is like a roaring lion tearing the prey, they have devoured people…" v26 "Her priests have violated My law and profaned My Holy things, they have not distinguished between the holy and the unholy…" v27 "Her leaders are like wolves tearing the prey ………to get dishonest gain."

Yet the Lord has a remnant people and He is calling them. They are people who love the Lord with all of their hearts. And as the day approaches that He is to return, they will begin to gather together. From all different back-grounds they will gather and have this in common, they simply hunger and thirst after His presence. If Christians would pass over into the Promised Land, into the most intimate chambers, they must be abandoned to the battle. It is time for the Church of Christ to arise and set their sights on entering into the manifest presence of God. They must be willing to lay down their lives, die to themselves and all of their fears if they are to enter that place where they will be engulfed in the flames of Shekinah glory. This is a higher place than miracles, although miracles will follow in the path of this new generation, but as an unintended consequence of the out flowing of God's presence. Like a mighty incoming tide the warriors will be swept into His presence. And as with every tide that flows in, it will flow out. And as we flow out on a tide of majestic reverence then we will take a portion of that glory back into the darkness of the world, a world that the Lord so loves.

13.

A LITTLE CHURCH HISTORY.

In order to understand better where we are as a Church it is important to understand where we came from and how we arrived at this place. Many Christians know a little of Constantine and that somehow after his seeming conversion the Church changed from being a persecuted Church to a persecuting church. In this chapter we will learn a little of church history from that period. What effect did the Emperor Constantine have on the church world then? And how does this affect the church today? And how does all of this relate to the remnant saints? What does it mean to be either a Kingdom saint, a pilgrim saint or remnant saint? All of these titles describe one person, the saint who walks in the Kingdom of God. They come from every tribe, every tongue and every nation. They cross denominational lines. Their identity is established in Christ, not in men or men's Kingdom. The walk of such a saint is often a lonely walk.

In every century down through the ages, beginning with the death and resurrection of Jesus, we see this saint. He is a lover of the Truth and would rather die than deny this truth. He would rather walk this world alone than compromise the truth. His country cannot shake it, his friends cannot shake it nor even his family because while he may love all of these passionately, nothing even comes close to his passion for the Truth. He has been captured by it, bought by it, ruined for the things of this world by it. Of course this truth of which I speak is the way, the truth and the life and no man comes to the Father except by Him, the Lord Jesus Christ, ruler of the Kingdom of God.

LOOKING BACK IN ORDER TO SEE AHEAD

Now I would like to take you to a time and place in history where this very parable plays out. It plays out in the larger sense. For while this parable of Jesus certainly applies to individuals first and foremost, it also applies to what claims to be the Church. The time is one not very many Christians know about. It is the time just prior to Constantine taking office. Now not many folks know too much about Constantine. Many know some myths about him, like he supposedly saw a cross in the sky prior to a battle and believed it was a sign from God and then went on to win the battle and convert to Christianity. Many also know this as a time when the Church changed from being a persecuted church to being part of the state, or as the time of the birth of the institutionalized Church, the merging of Church and State.

As you read on I want you to see why what happened during this period of time still affects us even till this day. And I want you to see why the Kingdom saint, the remnant saint, the pilgrim is such a threat to the institutional church. You will see that you are never more of a threat to the powers that be than when you expose them or shame them or reveal who they truly are (often by merely living a righteous life) This, of course is the effect that John the Baptist and Jesus had on the religious system of their day. They revealed many of them as mere men of the world, not lovers of God. These were men who were sold out to the kingdoms of this world and its power structure and their role within that power structure which gave them prominence, stature and a comfortable living.

They were not lovers of the Truth and when the right storm came along, and the enemy came at them like a flood, they were simply exposed for what they truly were and what they actually stood for, much of the time it would have been as much of a revelation to themselves as well as others. Once revealed though, they would become the mortal enemies of those who actually stood upon the solid Rock of Jesus and who are obedient to their King even though it cost them everything. Now it is important to note that not all men who were ever involved in the institutionalized church were wicked men of the world. There were layers upon layers of subtlety and it often took good men, men who had been transformed by the new birth, quite a journey to come out of her. As it was down through the centuries, so it still is today with many good men and women caught up in a system that was fatally flawed from the beginning and which is only truly revealed by a flood of evil.

The time I want to take you to is the period between 260 AD and 303 AD. Now this was a time or relative peace for the Church. There was still sporadic persecution, but on the whole, empire wide, this was a time of peace. Why is this time period so significant for us in the west today? Well in that time the Church became lax. The peace did not bring about a deepening of their faith, in fact quite the opposite. Theological debates raged. Now some were necessary of course, but in this time of peace they had the luxury of not having to deal with persecution. I would say that you the reader and I live in such times. It is beginning to change but nevertheless we in the west live in such times. We have had much more than forty years to become lukewarm and untested in our faith as a Body. For the saints living in 303AD it was all about to change, as I believe it is for the saints living today in the west.

Diocletian, emperor of Rome suddenly initiated the most severe persecution ever unleashed on the Body of Christ. It would last for eight years and was empire wide. The houses of prayer (some of which were church buildings, but most were homes) were burned to the ground, Christians were rounded up and suffered the most horrendous tortures ever seen and saints were killed by the tens of thousands. The period of peace prior to this had not served the church well, but many when faced with such horror stood firm and would not recant their faith, praise God. They would rather be tortured and killed than to deny the Truth that burned in them. Yet many more would deny the faith. They could not stand under this onslaught and their "faith" was simply swept away because their foundation was not Jesus. The parable that Jesus spoke in Luke 6 was coming to pass. Now this had happened on a smaller scale before at the turn of the third century and there had been a split then, I would encourage the readers to study the Novationists and the issues that they dealt with.

After eight long years, Diocletian finally gave up and in 311 he issued an edict of toleration. He had failed to wipe out Christianity. He actually asked Christians for their prayers, stepped down as Emperor and would later kill himself, a fitting end that many tyrants have come to in the annals of history. Now we come to Constantine. Shortly after he became a co-regent of Rome with Licinius. Licinius would rule in the east and Constantine the west. Constantine had a favorable disposition towards Christians. His region of influence during the persecution offered some comfort and shelter to Christians. So when he came to power, it would seem that God Himself must have been answering the prayers of the saints. Yet as David Bercot points out in his book The Kingdom That Turned the World Upside Down *"What the Church did not realize was that Satan had one more weapon in his arsenal: guile. If he and the world could not defeat the Kingdom, they would join it. Or rather they would cunningly entice the Christians to join them."*

This is a brilliant point by Bercot. He rightly identifies that Satan knows all too well the old adage that if you cannot beat them, join them. Or rather, as David points out, have them join you. Satan had tried to prevail against the Church by wiping them out, but the Kingdom saints, those whose foundation was Christ, stood upon a foundation that could not be moved no matter how severe the storm. But what of those who had not stood the test, what of those whose foundation was not Christ Himself but merely religion and vying for their own position here on this earth? What does it mean to be swept away? Can we liken that to a falling away? And once fallen but not dead, what do these deniers of the faith do when the storm passes? They build their own systems and churches, they build religion, a religion that will be stocked with once born men. And these once-born men will hate the twice-born man, the man that was born again into a Kingdom that cannot be shaken. The very existence of the twice- born man was and is and will be a constant source of, at best, irritation. At worse the once-born men hunt down and kill the twice- born man.

THE CONSTANTINE CONTAGION

Let us look at what kind of Kingdom Constantine built. You decide if he initiated and contaminated Christendom with a contagion that lasts until this day, that created the Catholic Church and also the reformed church. In 313 Constantine issued the Edict of Milan. This granted freedom of religion to all men, including Christians. I know that this may come as a shock to many American Christians, but yes, there was freedom of religion prior to some settlements in the colonies. Constantine went on and decreed that the properties stolen from Christians during the persecution would be returned. He also decreed that the houses of prayer that were burned would be rebuilt and paid for by the state. And even with that, Constantine was not finished. He decided in his earthly wisdom and undoubted friendliness towards those of the Christian faith that they should have very fine buildings in which to worship, very much larger structures since it was now the favored religion of the state. The previous modest houses of prayer would be too small to hold the large crowds that would now come, so he built them " churches," that were more ornate than the pagan temples of the day.

So we went from a faith that met in very modest houses of prayer to highly ornate temples of worship. We went from a faith that was persecuted by the state to a faith that was made an amalgam of the state. Constantine further recognized that most bishops and deacons lived on or near the poverty line. Now think about that saints-they lived on or near the poverty line. Now this was often by choice, men gladly giving up their estates, but nevertheless that is how most bishops and deacons lived prior to the great persecution of Diocletian. Now Constantine thought this most improper that men of the status of a bishop or a deacon should live in such a manner. So Constantine decided that the state would pay them a handsome salary. Think about it saints. Just a few years before Christendom had faced the most sever persecution it had ever experienced and now here was Constantine, building extravagant buildings called churches and paying bishops and deacons handsome salaries. A brilliant strategy of the Devil? Good cop bad cop syndrome with Diocletian and Constantine? I would argue that it could only have happened against the backdrop of such a great persecution. Prior to this men of God would not even take governmental roles never mind have the state pay for ornate buildings and receive a wage from them. One more thing, Constantine decreed that these churches did not have to pay property tax, which was one of the main ways Rome raised revenue.

Now how would the saints react to all of this? Well we soon see a split. And the split was basically along the lines of who stood firm during the persecution and those who did not. This would come to a head in a city in North Africa called Carthage. In that city, two groups developed. And much like the Novationists from 100 years prior, the Donatists did not care for not want to include in the Church those who had denied the faith during the great persecution. So we had two groups of leaders vying for control in Carthage. There were two sets of bishops and two sets of deacons. On the one side were the so-called Donatists, and on the other side the Catholics. So two groups but only one state/church building and only one set of salaries. Bercot writes "In the past, this controversy would have been purely an internal church matter. But Constantine's blessings to the church created a whole new issue. Which Bishop would receive the handsome salary offered by the State? Which Bishop and which group of presbyters would receive tax exemption? Which Bishop would have charge of the magnificent new church building that had been rebuilt at state expense?" (the Kingdom That Turned The World Upside Down, page 166)

It was eventually appealed to Constantine and he found in favor of the Catholics. The Catholics were established. Constantine even gifted the Lateran palace to them, which became the residence of the Popes for the next one thousand years. And of course from that point on every persecution that came against the true kingdom saints would come from, what Bercot calls a hybrid. The church which had formerly refused to take positions within the government, and had lived a humble and modest life, had been persecuted, now took roles within the state. They lived very well at the expense of the state and then became the persecutors of those Kingdom saints who will always be identified by their obedience to Jesus and their willingness to die rather than deny their faith. Rome and the church that had mostly denied their faith during the great persecution merged. And of course when Rome fell, the established church did not, it only became more powerful. This goes beyond anything that you would read in Lewis's "Screwtape Letters." This was quite simply, a brilliant plan by the deadliest foe of genuine Christianity, Satan.

WE ARE NOT IGNORANT OF HIS DEVICES.........ARE WE?

Now where does that leave the remnant saint today? How will the established church once again become so immersed in the state that they become one and then become the enemy of the Kingdom saints? When the world infiltrates and dominates the church then their concerns become one and the same. What threatens the world threatens the church and so they stand together to deal with the threat. What was born in the Constantine period has not changed, whether it was the Catholic Church or the schisms of the Reformation that would create state churches like the Church of England or the Lutheran church. We can see that the very same pattern has developed here in the United States, where the Evangelical church has become a very powerful political force. This is a vital part of any unholy alliance where the interests of the state merge and contaminate and overcome the church. This is the Constantine contagion.

Every institution that's root can be found and traced back to the Constantine period will not stand in that day. And what I mean by that is this. When the great evil that is soon to come upon us unfolds, many of those of the contagion will fall away, will be swept away, they will fall in line with the world. And many who now call us brothers, will soon be our persecutors. And why? Because neither the people nor their churches have built their lives or their organizations upon the Rock which is Jesus. Jesus plainly says that those who hear His Word and do not do it will fall and great will be the ruin of them. A structure or a life built on anything less than the Word of God and the carrying out of that word just simply cannot remain standing. It may take a month or several years, decades or even centuries but the Words of Jesus cannot be broken. Now just as the Kingdom saints all down through the ages have separated themselves from the evils of contaminated institutions and refused to be a part of them, so we see this happening again in our day. The time of peace is coming to an end for Christendom in the west. The great valley of decision lies ahead for those who call themselves after the name of Jesus. In that valley lies persecution and blasphemy and men who do not heed the words of Jesus. Who will stand?

Those who will stand are those who love the Lord Jesus more than they love their country, more than they love their culture, more than they love their friends, more than they love even their own families. They love Jesus more than a comfortable life and more than what this world has to offer. Those who will stand are the pilgrim saints, the sojourners, the remnant. They will stand because they are already dead to this world and alive to the Kingdom of God in which they already walk. Twice- born saints, now born into a Kingdom that was and is and is to come. They serve the King of this Kingdom with all of their hearts. They always have, they do now and they always will. This is the eternal Kingdom of God and no amount of persecution can change that, all it can do is reveal who is the Kingdom saint and who is not.

14.

A FUNDAMENTAL SHIFT

There is a fundamental shift taking place in our world. God is preparing His children for a paradigm shift in attitude towards them. For many generations in the west there has been a general accepting attitude of Christianity.

And He said to them, when I sent you without purse and wallet and sandals, did you lack anything? And they said, nothing. And He said to them, but now, he who has a purse, let him take it, and likewise his wallet. And he who has no sword, let him sell his garment and buy one. Luke 22:35-36

When Jesus sent out His Disciples by 2s, they encountered many blessings and walked in the miraculous. So much so that Jesus had to remind them sternly that they were not to rejoice in the fact that they had power over demons or signs and wonders but they were to rejoice in their salvation, a fact lost on many today. Salvation is always the focus of those who truly follow Jesus. Now in Luke 22 we see Jesus preparing His disciples for a sea change in attitude towards them. No longer would they find a warm and accepting grateful people, in fact quite the opposite.

Now why was this? Well Jesus was about to suffer and die. The battle was about to intensify. Death and hell was about to suffer its ultimate defeat. That was the spiritual battle and we are facing the same battle today. Jesus is coming back. He is at the door. The enemy knows that His time is short and he is gathering all the forces of hell for his last great battle. We are now living in the relative calm before the storm here in the west. In the rest of the world the battle is already raging and our brothers and sisters are being slaughtered and persecuted.

Now why did the people's attitude towards the disciples change and what can we learn from that today? Up until Jesus reveals His true purpose here on earth, the general population of Israel had always believed that when Messiah came He would restore Israel to its rightful place. He would establish Gods Kingdom here on earth and they would be the rulers of it and the Romans would be destroyed, their oppressors would be judged and defeated. And along comes Jesus and he walks in the miraculous power that only God could walk in. He heals the sick and He delivers the demon possessed. He speaks with a wisdom and authority that could only come from God. The people rejoice in Him, and would even make Him their King. We witness that as He rode into Jerusalem on a donkey.

Now when he was in Jerusalem at the pass-over, in the feast day, many believed in his name, when they saw the miracles which he did. But Jesus did not commit himself unto them, because he knew all men, and needed not that any should testify of man: for he knew what was in man. Joh 2:23-25

What did Jesus know? Why would Jesus not commit Himself to these "believers?" What was in these men that was diametrically opposed to Jesus even though they openly believed in Him? He knew that once they found out that He had come to suffer and die that they would reject that message. Everything was great while He healed them and delivered them and fed them and gave them insight into heavenly things, yet when he revealed that He had come to suffer and die, in fulfilment of Isa 53, they not only rejected Him, they were the ones who cried out for His blood. An insight into this can be seen in one of the chief Apostles, Peter.

From that time Jesus began to show His disciples that He must go to Jerusalem and suffer many things from the elders and chief priests and scribes, and be killed, and be raised again the third day. Then Peter took Him and began to rebuke Him, saying, God be gracious to You, Lord! This shall never be to You. But He turned and said to Peter, Go, Satan! You are an offense to Me, for you do not savor the things that are of God, but those that are of men. Then Jesus said to His disciples, if anyone desires to come after Me, let him deny himself and take up his cross and follow Me. For whoever desires to save his life shall lose it, and whoever desires to lose his life for My sake shall find it. Mat 16:20-25

Brothers and sisters we live in a day and age where the notion of suffering for His sake has become repulsive. We live in a day and age in the west where most profess to be believers. We have already seen that Jesus refused to commit Himself to believers who only followed Him because of the miracles that they saw and for what they could get from Him. Jesus was and is looking for a people who would take up their cross and follow after Him and join Him in His sufferings and death. We are soon to see this fundamental shift in Christendom. The majority, who in one fashion or another have been and seek to live their best lives now, will react just as Peter reacted, just as the "believers" of Jesus day reacted, they will soundly reject any notion of suffering for the sake of Jesus and then they will turn on those who do embrace it.

Persecution is coming. Jesus is coming. The majority will reject the true calling of Christianity. It will be repulsive to them. They will turn on those who embrace the true Christ and who follow the narrow path. Yet for those who embrace the cross, the narrow path, who follow Jesus they will be empowered from on high. He equips those He calls. He does not leave nor forsake His children. God will pour out His Spirit upon His children and they will walk in His power. And so the question becomes "why are you following Jesus?" The dividing line will be between those who mind the things of men and those who mind the things of God. God is revealing to His people all over the world that they must suffer for His sake. To those of us in the West, this is a fundamental shift. How shall we react? God knows what is in a man. He is shaking everything that can be shaken. He is sifting believers prior to His coming. There can be no middle ground, no neutrality. You cannot have one foot in the world and one foot in His Kingdom. You will either love the brethren and take your place with them as they suffer for His sake or you will call for their blood. It is coming brothers and sister. It is time to embrace the cross. Those who do will walk in resurrection power, the power of the Living God. Those who do not will become enemies of God and His people.

We live in perilous times.

As the Lord approaches, as we enter into the times of sorrow, as the birth pangs are beginning that marks the imminent rise of the anti-christ and therefore the return of our Lord and Saviour, we must be on guard and heed the warnings of the Word of God. Jesus plainly told us to beware of the leaven of the Pharisees and of Herod. (Mar 8:15)

Pharisees and Sadducees

Now the leaven here is plainly speaking of false doctrine. And so it is helpful to know who opposed Jesus and why. For the same spirits that opposed Jesus (we do not wrestle against flesh and blood) are still alive and well and will oppose Jesus, in His followers, and all the more so as that day approaches. So those who opposed Jesus were the Pharisees, the Sadducees and the Herodians. As we describe who they are, you must discern who represents these groups today and see if the motivations which existed in the days of Jerusalem, still exist today. I would argue that they do and that the battle will be the same, just set against a different backdrop.

First we have the Pharisees and the Sadducees. Now they had been enemies of each other in one shape or another for centuries, dating back to post exilic days. The Sadducees were of the priestly class and were wealthy and aristocratic. The Pharisees came from a much poorer background and therefore carried the favor of the common people who made up the majority. The Sadducees were very much "Hellenized" meaning they were greatly influenced by Greek culture which was the predominant philosophy of much of that region. The Pharisees resisted that greatly. Much of today's Christendom has been Hellenized, meaning of course that it has been so influenced by the world that it looks just like the world. The fundamentalists try to hold back this tide of worldliness just as the Pharisees did in their days.

Another difference between these two groups was that the Sadducees greatly emphasized the importance of the second temple and all the rites and services that went along with it, while the Pharisees emphasized the importance of the Mosaic Law. Also, the two groups were in complete disagreement when it came to an afterlife. The Sadducee rejected that notion while the Pharisee fully embraced the notion of life after death. So as you can see, on multiple levels, whether cultural or class or religious, these groups were on very different pages.

Herodians

Now the Herodians were also a sect of the Jews who were the political class and were obviously followers of Herod or the Herodian dynasty, the puppet kings of the Romans. They were more closely aligned with the Sadducees. And so we see the Herodians and the Sadducees and the Pharisees coming together to bring about the downfall of Jesus. These were groups that were diametrically opposed to each other in deep-rooted issues, but for reasons we will speak to, found enough common ground to come together to not only oppose Jesus, but demand His death. (Matt 22:16, Mar 3:6, Mar 12:13) So we see an unholy alliance of the politicians, the fundamentalists and the priests.

COMMON ENEMY MAKES FOR STRANGE BEDFELLOWS

Even although all these groups were very much divided on these deep-rooted issues, where did they find common ground? Well all of them greatly benefited from the Temple system of worship. This was the money-maker of the day. Today's equivalent is Christendom itself and the established system that we have in place. Of course in the midst of all of that they had a delicate balancing act to play with the Romans. The Romans at any time, and at the whim of any mad emperor, could destroy their whole system overnight. None of this was lost to any of the groups we have been talking about. Now the money generated by the temple system and the hierarchy of power was the key to the survival of the whole system.

It turned out that those with a vested interest in the system itself were not as divided as they may have thought they were. When the system that gave all of these groups their status, their standard of living, their reputations and their total livelihood came under threat, then they came together to deal with that threat. It turned out that they idolized the system so much that when Jesus stood in the midst of them, the one for whom the temple was built, they not only did not recognize and reject Him, they came together and sought how they could kill him.

2Ti 3:1 *"This know also, that in the last days perilous times shall come."* Brothers and sisters we are in the last days and perilous times are upon us. The forces that came against Jesus and the saints of the early church, the forces that have hunted down our brothers and sisters down through the centuries are gathering for a last great offensive against the children of the light. These forces have always been an amalgam of Pharisees, Sadducees and Herodians and the state. If we are to look for a clue as to who the Pharisees and Sadducees of our days are we must look to Scripture. In John 8 and starting in verse 31 we see Jesus talking to "believing" Jews. Now I want you to think of believing Christians, professing Christians of our day as we consider what Jesus says to them and how they reply. He says *"If ye continue in my word, then are ye my disciples indeed; And ye shall know the truth, and the truth shall make you free.* (John 8:31,32)

Now, have not the prophetic voices of our age, Tozer, Sparks, Ravenhill, to name but a few, have they not urged professing Christians in the West that they must live and be led by the word of God if they desire to be free and to be true disciples? To come forward at an altar and make a confession is nothing if there are no fruits of repentance. If the Lord sets a man free then He is free indeed, not theologically but actually. And how do we determine that freedom? Well we shall know them by their fruits shall we not? What man or woman of God would not rejoice to hear these words from the Lord's own lips?

Let's see how these believers reacted to this simple command from the Lord. *They answered Him, "We are Abraham's seed and were never in bondage to anyone. How do you say, You will be made free?"* (John 8:33) You see how blinded they were? They were insulted by the notion that they were not free. They look to their national heritage and fall back upon their founding Father, Abraham. They say to Jesus that they have never been in bondage to anyone. Now obviously the kind of freedom that Jesus was talking about had nothing to with national freedom. He had not come to release them from the bondage of the Romans. Before the chapter is finished Jesus tells them their father is the devil and they pick up stones to kill Him, bear in mind this is "believers."

ARE WE FREE?

What about believers here in America? If Jesus spoke to them and told them that if they wanted to be free and be genuine disciples then they must abide in His word, what would they say? What do they think of when they think of freedom? Is the freedom that they worship and idolize the freedom that Jesus was talking about? Can Americans claim that they are not in bondage? Would the average American believer be insulted if you were to challenge their life-styles and tell them that they are in bondage and if they would be free they must abide in His word? Now please don't get this wrong, Jesus is not compelling the believers to read and memorize Scriptures, He is saying that they must "continue" in His word if they were to be His disciples.

Continue in it, abide in it, dwell in it, it must dwell in them. The life of Christ must dwell in them and this is not a one-time thing, it is a continuous action which is proven by the lives that men live. And while none of us know the secrets of the heart, we can know the actions of men. And if men are not dwelling in and living in and walking in the commands of God then Jesus Himself says that they cannot be His disciples. How this flies in the face of hyper grace teachings of the day and other false teachings. Beware of the leaven of the Pharisees.

Now if a man is not an abider in the life of Christ, in His words and in His commands, if he is a law unto himself and follows his own ways and ways that seem right unto him, then he is a religious man. For the men that Paul describes in 2Tim 3, the men of the last days which are perilous are men who are *"ever learning and never able to come to the full knowledge of the truth."* (2Ti 3:7) They are Pharisees and Sadducees and Herodians. They are an unholy alliance of religious and political men. And despite their seemingly great differences, they will come together in these last perilous days and be a common enemy to the true saints who will tell them straightly that not only do they know nothing of true freedom, but that the political freedoms that they enjoy, their position within the system that they themselves have built, is under judgement and that God will come against them for they do not know Him.

THE WOLVES COME FROM WITHIN – JANNES & JAMBRES

And so brothers and sisters, the first eight verses of 2Tim chapter 3 are speaking not of the world but of Christendom. And the final two names, Jannes and Jambres are noted as men who greatly resisted Moses and since the context of this chapter is perilous last days, then we can assume that men like Jannes and Jambres will greatly resist God's true people in these latter days. Now who were these men and what do they represent today? Well Jannes and Jambres are reckoned to be two of the occultist magicians in Pharaoh's court who replicated the rod turning into a snake, then were able to replicate some of the plagues. It is reckoned that when Moses and the children of Israel left Egypt that they had become followers of Moses, perhaps for the same reasons as Simon the magician of Acts 8, who was amazed at the power of the Apostles and who tried to buy this power.

Extra Biblical evidence suggests that Jannes and Jambres were very influential in persuading Aaron to make a golden calf when it seemed that Moses may not return. And we know that the calf was made with the gold and the treasure that was taken from Egypt. And so we see two men who had some kind of power, perhaps even a form of Godliness since they were now following Moses, persuade men to fall down and worship the treasures of the world and act just like the world from which they had been delivered. Do we not see that in Christendom today? There are so many men just like Jannes, just like Jambres, just like Simon, men who are desperate to operate in the power of God so that they can impress others and elevate their own status. It will never happen. Today's so-called miracle workers and self-proclaimed prophets are merely operating in the soulish realm. And God's fire will never fall on them. This will be one reason they will hate genuine saints, for as God pours out His Spirit on genuine saints in these latter times and they begin to move in the genuine power of God, it will enrage the false teachers just as it enraged the religious leaders in the days of Jesus. We see a small clue in Matthew 27:18 as to why they wanted Jesus dead... *"For he knew they had delivered Him because of envy."*

REPROBATES, CASTAWAYS AND FRIENDS OF THE WORLD

Worshippers of the gold and the treasures of this world. What does Paul say about such men? He says that they are *"men of corrupt minds, reprobate concerning the faith."* (2 Tim 3:8) This word reprobate means "to be castaway, rejected." Yes indeed , these men are believers, and we can see them in every branch of Christianity today, whether it is the Word of Faith people, the Prosperity people or those who are obsessed with the power of God and would buy it with money if they could so as to dazzle the crowd. And they are joined by the liberal dead denominations and the dead fundamentalists. And can I tell you brothers and sisters, just like the Pharisees and the Sadducees and the Herodians, they are all part of the one system and they will come together at some point and will be the deadliest enemies of the true saint. You see, they worship the world and the things of the world, this is their heart. God will expose their hearts in the coming days as their loyalties to the world and all it offers will become more and more apparent. Today it is the homosexual issue and they will relent on that because they are ultimately friends of the world. Soon it will be the name of Jesus and the truth that He and He alone is the only way to heaven. This is and will become increasingly more unacceptable to the world so when the world demands it, they will relent on that too.

Remember, the Pharisees and the Sadducees and the Herodians were not allowed to just quietly hand Jesus over, no, their whole hearts were exposed when they cried out *"We have no King but Caesar."* You see Jesus was not their God, their God was the god of this world just as in John 8 where Jesus tells the "believers" that their father is the devil. (John 8:42) And so these groups in conjunction with the state will one day in the relatively near future, demand the blood of the saints who at no point will turn away from the Word of God and will continue to be led by His Spirit. God trains His children. He has been refining His own all the way along. He has led them through many trials and tribulations and deserts, He has been preparing His children to face such a day.

And of course in 2 Tim 3 Paul not only identifies all the reprobates, the rejected and the castaway, he also identifies the walk of the true saint. On the one hand you will recognize the reprobate because he chases after and worships the treasure of this world and plays, just as the world plays. He is constantly seeking the power of God for his own ends yet God will never fall in power upon such men and their gatherings. On the other hand we have the true saint. How can we identify the true saint? *Persecutions, afflictions, which came unto me at Antioch, at Iconium, at Lystra; what persecutions I endured: but out of them all the Lord delivered me. Yea, and all that will live godly in Christ Jesus shall suffer persecution* (2 Ti 3:11, 12)

IF CHRISTIANITY WAS A CRIME, WOULD THERE BE ENOUGH EVIDENCE TO CONVICT YOU?

The true saint picks up his cross and dies daily to his flesh. He has encountered God in such a fashion that his life is a witness to the world, not his words, his life. The true saint's words and life are in harmony. He is not perfect, this he knows but his life is a witness to his God. He has learned to be content in every situation. He knows that Godliness with contentment is great gain. This is the kind of gain he rejoices in. When He suffers for His Lord he rejoices in that as well, for he has been counted worthy to enter into His sufferings. He counts all loss as rubbish but rather he rejoices to be found in Him, to know Him more deeply. He despairs as he sees preachers go to enormous lengths to assure "nominal Christians" that their sinful lives are no great problem, they have the magicians potion, cheap grace. The kind of grace that does not require your whole heart nor does it require you to pick up your cross, it only requires your attendance and your money to enhance and further their own kingdoms.

Brothers and sisters, what does the man and woman of God do and how does it fly in the face of what passes for much of Christianity today? He chooses *"Rather to suffer affliction with the people of God, than to enjoy the pleasures of sin for a season; esteeming the reproach of Christ greater riches than the treasures in Egypt; for he was looking for the reward. By faith he left Egypt, not fearing the wrath of the king, for he endured as seeing Him who is invisible."* (Heb 11:25-27)

What will you choose? The riches of Egypt? A season of pleasurable sin? Or will you be counted with Christ and live Godly in Christ Jesus and suffer persecution? This is the choice that is before Christendom today. Evil men and seducers have certainly increased, just as Paul prophesied in this chapter from Timothy. And many have been deceived, indeed the deceivers are themselves deceived. Oh what a horrendous shock when they come before the living God and cry out to Him about all that they have done in His name and then they hear these most dreadful of words *"depart from me workers of iniquity , for I never knew you."*

15.

CHRISTENDOM HAS LOST ITS WAY?

Modern day Christianity has lost its way, has lost its focus. The central truths upon which we have stood for two thousand years has been lost in a fog of noise and distraction and in the rise of humanism and the flesh. Never before, in the history of the Western world have we seen such an indulgent, entitlement-minded people. And since a great majority of Christendom is just like the world, then we see an indulgent, entitlement-minded church. These people have produced preachers and teachers that will tell them what they want to hear. It is often hard to tell the difference between a motivational speaker and a preacher. Instead of teaching and preaching based upon the central truths of Christianity, there is preaching and teaching on how to get the most out of life. They teach that God would never call you to something that you do not like. Can you imagine your kids telling you that they are not going to do their chores that you have set for them because it does not bring them pleasure? Would you indulge your kids in this behavior? Or would you take the time to explain to them about building character, about sacrifice and about servant-hood? Are these three elements some of the things that are missing from the church? It's strange that Christendom would condemn the "If it feels good, do it" generation yet at the same time teach this from their own pulpits.

This is the message from the cross less preachers. This is really the only message they can preach to the many who are living for the flesh, for the moment, for themselves. This message answers the cry of the flesh which is always seeking its own and yet never produces satisfaction. And the more Christendom panders to their own flesh and desires, the more worldly they become. The irony is that the few who find the narrow path which is death to self, picking up one's cross, denying the flesh, these few become more

Christ like and know what it is to be content in every situation. True preachers of the Word will show you how to die to this world and live for the next.

The hirelings will show you, by example, how to live for this world and not for the next. They will show you by their $2000 suits and their $700 shoes. Some will boast of these things from the pulpit. They will proudly tell you that they drive a BMW and so should you. They say that this is God's will for you, that you should live your best life now. Apparently living your best life now includes looking worldly and indulging and fulfilling that which brings you pleasure and living out what you believe you are entitled to. This is not the message of the Cross and the Gospel. This crass message will only continue to alienate Christendom from reaching out to the un-churched. As God deals with an indulgent and entitlement generation will your message be the message of the Cross and how the Lord suffered and died and rose again so that they could find life, despite their circumstances?

So what should our focus be as Christians? What is the central truth upon which we stand? The three pillars of foundational truth are 1. He came. 2. He died. 3. He rose again. We celebrate these truths as Christians. We know that He is no longer a baby in a manger and we also know that He is no longer hanging upon the Cross. He is sitting at the right hand of the Father. He dwells within us. That is the Kingdom of God, it dwells within us. These are the central truths of Christianity. If Jesus is no longer on the cross, if He is resurrected in power and by His life gives life, then why should our focus be on a cross that Jesus no longer hangs from? Why is it important to remember the cross? If the resurrection is our present reality and the power of our lives, what does it empower us to do?

The living Jesus empowers us to die. The cross is the symbol of sacrifice and death. To live for Him is to die to ourselves and the world. In the Spiritual we came, we died and we rose again as a new creature in Christ. As we move towards and become like Jesus, we die to ourselves. And so there is an important intertwining of dying to ourselves and living the resurrected life. It is the heads and the tails of the same coin. If you focus on just one aspect to the detriment of the other, you will become imbalanced in your walk. We surely must pick up our cross daily it is important to realize that this will produce an abundant spiritual life in Christ and while you may die to the flesh internally, the world should see your joy expressed externally and wonder and marvel how such a thing could be. This is pleasing to God.

The proof of our new life, our resurrection from the dead, our authentic faith is not a large house or a $2000 suit or a prosperous life in this world, these things prove nothing in the Spiritual. The proof of our faith is how we react to carrying our cross. In the midst of death to ourselves does the love of Jesus pour forth? Do we minister to others when we ourselves are in the midst of trial and testing's? Have we found the secret of being content in every situation? The cross does not lie. There is no hypocrisy on the cross. Tozer said that you knew one thing about a man carrying a cross out of the city, you knew he was not coming back. The cross signifies death to self and death to the world. It's only by taking up our cross that we can crucify the flesh. The flesh wars against the Spirit. The flesh must die, it dies only upon the cross, it thrives on indulgence.

The walk of the cross is a lonely walk. Yet in every generation, across denominational lines, brothers and sisters will be called out. They will know each other when they meet. They will be people who have rejected the "norm." They will be a people who are seeking a deeper walk with Jesus. While the crowd run after the latest craze and those that tickle their ears, these people will find themselves on an ancient narrow path. This path begins at Calvary and ends at the throne. It is a very difficult and lonely path but all the saints who have come before you have walked this very path. Be encouraged today saints, God has seen and sees the afflictions of His people. He has not left us as orphans, we have the Holy Spirit who can take us to a place that Jesus has prepared for us. He is our high tower and the righteous can run into it and are safe. There is a place beneath His wings that is ours. He has given us wings in the Spiritual so that we can fly to this place. And in this prepared place we can discover joy where there should be no joy. We can discover peace where there should be no peace. We can discover love where hate should be. We can be fed although a famine has overtaken the land. He is our fountain in a land that is dry and dusty, in a land where there is no water.

As the spiritual famine deepens, as the drought begins to change the landscape, as the counterfeit increases daily, the Lord knows how to feed His children. As the storm that rages then the Lord says to His children "I am the eye of the storm, do not be afraid of it, walk into the heart of it and find peace at the center it, I am the Lord of all storms and I stand in the midst of them and beckon unto my own to come unto me and take my hand and I will lead you through and you will not be overcome or destroyed." We praise the Lord today that He sees all things and He knows all things and to those who have taken up their cross and walk the narrow path He is their strength and their comfort and sustainer.

Christendom has despised Jesus

Now I realize that this is a provocative title, I make no apologies for that. In 2 Sam 12, we find King David in a very bad situation. He has committed adultery with Bathsheba, he tried to cover his tracks when she got pregnant, but a foreign convert , Uriah the Hittite , the husband of Bathsheba was more honorable that David. Therefore David's attempts to cover up his adultery was foiled so David had him killed.

Brothers and sisters, this is such a low state for the man after God's own heart. And after Nathan the prophet comes to David and exposes him, God speaks. God speaks brothers and sisters, one should be very afraid when God speaks, it is a fearful thing to fall into the hands of the Living God. And here is the charge that God levels against David, His beloved. *"You have despised me."* (1 Sam 12:10) Can you imagine hearing that charge against you from God? Yet that is exactly what David heard.

Now this word despised in the Greek is "baw-zaw" meaning to disesteem, to think lightly off. It is the same word used in Gen 25:34 to describe Esau's selling of his birthright for some bread and some soup. Can you imagine selling your birthright just simply to satisfy your immediate needs? Can you imagine that food on the table would be thought more highly of than the Living God and the birthright that He has given to us? And yet, do we not live in a day and age where our immediate needs, meaning the basic needs of this world and our day-to-day living are thought of more highly than God? Are we not encouraged to live our best lives now? Have we not allowed our desires and hungers to be elevated above our love and desire for God? And are we not blind to it, so terribly blind to it? If David needed a prophet to reveal his wickedness, and this a man after God's own heart, beloved of God, are we so proud as to think that we would not need this level of rebuke?

We are that blind, Christendom is that blind and in fact has never been more blind to its state. So the question we have to ask ourselves is Christendom today representative of Esau or David? It's a hugely important question. As soon as God finishes speaking to David, rebuking him, David says this *"I have sinned against the Lord."* (2 Sam 12:13) We see humility in David as the prophet tells him that by his actions God is blasphemed by His enemies. And because of that humility, David is forgiven, not without consequences, but forgiven none-the-less. The very next thing we here about Esau after he had despised his birthright is that he marries two women outside of the faith so to speak, he marries two Hittites strangely enough. He is doubling down on his sin and fully immersing himself in the world.

Christendom today has despised God in the fullest sense of that word. They are as blind to their sin as David was. And unless they hear God directly and acknowledge and repent of their sin as David did, they will be hopelessly lost to, and be entangled by the cares of this world. In describing what is and what is not the Kingdom of God Jesus says this

"And the cares of this world, and the deceitfulness of riches, and the lusts of other things entering in, choke the word, and it becometh unfruitful........For there is nothing hidden which shall not be revealed; nor became covered, but that it might come to the light. If any man has ears to hear, let him hear." (Mar 4:19-23)

So Father I pray in the mighty name of Jesus our Lord, that Christendom, all that calls itself by thy name and has caused your enemies to blaspheme you, shall hear the word of God as David heard and be broken and contrite before your throne for despising you. For despising their birthright and allowing the cares of this world and their immediate needs to overshadow you Lord, may they find forgiveness rather than further entanglement with this world which will surely choke them to death. Lord you lay before us life and death, may we all reach out and take a hold of life, eternal life and may we despise, think lightly of the things of this world for they are surely passing away and before very long we shall all stand before you. We pray this in the name of Jesus.

16.

THOSE WHO SOW WITH TEARS.....

Since the beginning of time, there has been this question, or some form of it "Why do bad things happen to good people?" Some philosophers have asked "What is justice?" Now Christians are not immune to these thoughts or questions, in fact I would argue, that we will all ask that question to one degree or another at some point in our walk, maybe at many points in our walk.

Now there are certain times in our life when it is not just one bad thing that happens. Sometimes they overlap don't they? They threaten to overwhelm us and those initial questions are simply intensified as we try to figure out what is going on and what is the purpose of it all. Many of you will readily identify with these times. They are specific times when the enemy comes in like a flood and threatens to drown us in our circumstances. We scramble in our minds to make sense of it all. We hear familiar Scriptures from our hearts reminding us that God will never leave us nor forsake us yet that is exactly how we feel, left and forsaken and then the hammer drops again.

Can I suggest that life, the Christian life, whether you know it or not is an all-out battle. There is an enemy of your soul and he does seek to drown you, he does seek to simply sweep you away by wave after wave of circumstances. It is in these times that we make life altering decisions. Now remember the enemy is after your testimony, make no mistake about that. He does not care about you at all, what he wants you to do is to curse God and die. He wants others to see, as they look upon your circumstances, merely a man or a woman just like them. He wants to steal hope from your heart. He wants to present you as hopeless to the world so that a hopeless world can take comfort from the fact that there is really nothing in what you have said in the past, that it was merely all words and now circumstances have revealed that you are no different from them.

He wants to rob you of your peace, he wants to show the world that the peace that you claimed to have was merely circumstantial peace, not a supernatural peace that surpasses understanding. He wants to present you to the world as just like them and that as long as things are going okay then you have peace, but as soon as you are opposed by trial and circumstance, then your peace is gone, just like the worlds. He wants to rob you of your joy. He wants to show the world that this joy that you had was not supernatural, but merely a happiness that the world understands which again is gleaned from circumstances. He does not want the world to see the kind of joy that Paul presents after having been scourged and thrown into a dungeon and yet begins to praise God in the darkness of the night. And in that incident we see that this kind of joy, this supernatural joy is a door that leads from the deepest valleys, the darkest nights, the most gruesome of circumstances into the throne room of God Himself and that open door allows the power of God to flow into that very darkness and convince those who dwell in that darkness that there is a light that can redeem them from their chains.

In 1 Sam 30 we see David in a season when he could have asked the questions that we asked in the opening of this chapter. David has done no wrong. He had been watching the sheep of his father when the prophet of God comes along and anoints him. He has acted valiantly on the battle field for the sake of God. He has killed giants and overwhelmed the enemies of Gods people and brought victory after victory. He has been loyal to King Saul and the family of Saul. Yet here in 1 Sam 30 we see David in one of his many low points in life, where circumstances have multiplied and come against him, where a set of circumstances that cannot seem to get worse, do. You see brothers and sisters, we shall be challenged many times in our lives. That is a fact. Whether you know it or not, there is a raging battle and it is the enemy's full-time task to tear down the witness of Jesus in the earth. And so here is David, having had to flee from his home and family with Saul hunting him down like a dog and now even the Philistines want nothing to do with him because they do not trust him. He returns to the town where he lived, Ziklag, undoubtedly very dejected, and what does he find? The town has been burned down and all the wives and the children have been taken. Now I can hear David's cry now "Lord, have I not had enough?" Sorrow has piled upon sorrow and it threatens to crush David and those who follow him, so much so that even those who have followed him begin to turn on him.

"Then David and the people who were with him lifted up their voices and wept until they had no more power to weep."(1 Sam 30:4) Have you been there brothers and sisters? Maybe some of you are there now? Now what are we to do? It says "But David strengthened himself in the Lord his God." There is no rebuke for his tears, in fact it is quite a thing to weep until you have not even the strength left to weep, and maybe you have done that. Yet David does something that he will be called upon to do many more times in his walk with the Lord, he "strengthened himself in the Lord." Now that phrase "strengthened himself" in the Greek is khaw-zak and it means to bind, to restrain to conquer. You see we are called to overcome. It also means to hold fast, to maintain, to be steadfast, resolute and prevail. We cannot possibly see the bigger picture, God sees it all, He sits upon the circle of the earth, He sees our lives from beginning to end. He sees at this moment that David will prevail, he sees that he will pursue, and by His hand he will overcome. David does not know that because he cannot see that, he must trust God that God knows. He will have to do this time and again in his walk, and he does and he overcomes.

We see the clues and the insight in overcoming in one of David's psalms, 40. "I waited patiently for the Lord and He inclined to me and heard my cry." We must wait upon the Lord and believe that the Lord not only sees our situations but that he sees our tears and hears our cries. "He also brought me up out of a horrible pit. Out of the miry clay and set my feet upon a Rock and established my steps." You see, He hears and He sees and for those who trust in Him and wait upon Him, He delivers them from very dark places and He establishes them once again on solid ground where once they were sinking and drowning in a quick sand of despair and hopelessness. The tears must give way to hope and trust. After the tears end there must be a resolution in us to wait upon the Lord. In this we exercise our faith in God and this pleases God and confounds the enemy's schemes. David comes upon his enemies and finds them having a party, rejoicing in their great victory but they had not reckoned upon the God of David and in God, David overcomes.

David can then say , having gone through the gamut of hopelessness and despair and so many tears that *"Blessed is that man who makes the Lord his trust.......I delight to do your will , O God and your law is written within my heart."* Jesus is seated on the throne of the hearts of every saint. It is this fact that brings us through every trial and every tribulation. It is because of our love for Him that when all our tears have been shed that we will rise from that place and bind and restrain the thoughts of self-pity and defeat. We will arise resolute and steadfast and we will prevail and overcome because He who sits on the throne of our hearts was Himself resolute and steadfast when He arose from His own tears and agony in Gethsemane. He arose having acknowledged the will of His Father and set His face towards Calvary and beyond. We too, who love the Lord will do this by the power and might of the Holy Spirit that magnifies the Lord Jesus who sits upon the circle of our heart and sees.

Behold the Lamb of God

To every-thing there is a season and a time for every purpose under the heavens: A time to be born, a time to die, a time to plant and a time to pull up what is planted; a time to kill, and a time to heal, a time to break down and a time to build up; a time to weep and a time to laugh, a time to mourn and a time to dance; a time to throw away stones and a time to gather stone together; a time to embrace and a time to refrain from embracing; a time to get and a time to lose, a time to keep and a time to throw away; a time to tear and a time to sew, a time to keep silence and a time to speak; a time of war and a time to make peace; a time to love and a time to hate. (Ecc 3:1-8)

This is the season for God's remnant people to glorify God. The focus of God's people must be to glorify Him in the assembly of the people. As His people glorify Him, God will step down. He will not step down to justify a man's ministry or a man's ability to teach, He will step down when the people seek Him with their whole hearts. Sunday after Sunday, our hour long services are apportioned up and we expect God to respond, we expect God to step down in His apportioned 20 minutes or so. He will not do it.

In order to truly glorify God we must understand who He is and who we are in Christ. No army marches into battle with their heads hung low. When the army of God arrays itself for battle it must come to the battle with its head raised high to the heavens with eyes that gaze on the wonder of God. So I would say to every remnant believer, all who have mourned the state of the church and the state of the world, close your ears to that robber of hope, to that deceiver of the saints. He is the accuser of the brethren who has lied and whispers in your ears "If the foundations be destroyed, what can the righteous do?" The foundations of this world may shake in the midst of mighty earthquakes. The foundations of our homes may be swept away by fire and by flood but the solid foundations of our Lord and Saviour Jesus shall never be shaken and shall never be destroyed. As we focus on God and glorify Him, let us speak this to the enemy of our souls "Behold the Lamb of God that taketh away the sins of the world."

Behold the Righteous One, behold Him that is glorious in majesty. Behold Him that is pure in Holiness. Behold Him that was and is and is to come and evermore shall be. Behold the Son of Glory. Behold Him who was lifted up and now is high and lifted up. Behold Him who is worthy to open the Book. Behold the Lamb of God who was slain before the foundations of the earth were established. Behold Him who is faithful and true. Behold Him who is the fullness of the Godhead. Behold Him who leads the armies of heaven to victory over all the powers of darkness. Behold Him who has conquered hell and death and sin and all the powers of the grave. Behold Him who was dead but is alive and seated at the right hand of the Father. Yes we say behold the Lamb of God who taketh away the sins of the world and dwells forevermore in the midst of the throne. Behold the Lamb as the angels cry holy, holy, holy is our Lord and our God in whom there is no shadow and in whom dwells no darkness. Behold the mercy of God. Behold the justice of God. Behold the righteousness of God. Behold Gods judgment and behold His love.

Behold the Lamb of God that taketh away the sins of the world. Behold, if the Spirit of the one who was raised from the dead dwells in you shall He not also make your mortal bodies alive by His Spirit? For as many as are led by the Spirit of God are sons of God. We do not have a spirit of bondage so that we may dwell in fear but are adopted sons of the living God who can cry out to God and call Him Father. And the Holy Spirit of the living God bears witness in the very depths of our souls that we are His children, praise God. And of course, that majestic truth leads to the truth that since we are His children, then we are His heirs, indeed joint heirs with Christ. And as we enter into His sufferings we count our present trials as mere rubbish in comparison to the coming glory that God Himself will reveal in us. For we have been pre-destined to be conformed to the image of His Son Jesus. This the enemy knows well. It is his full-time occupation to have the saints question themselves and doubt their standing before God. Did not that old serpent, that father of lies even try this with Jesus? He says "If indeed you are the Son of God." Even his question is an accusation and a deliberate lie for Satan knew well that he stood before the Son of the Living God.

So we do not listen to the enemy across the field of battle who shouts lies and curses at the remnant people of God. We listen to the promises in the Word of the Living God as He leads His children into battle. He says that He has multiplied grace and peace to us according to His divine power because He knows us and we know Him. Not as the world knows Him, we know Him in the depths of our spirits and the Spirit bears witness to that. And He has promised that we would partake of His divine nature having escaped the corruption of this world. These things are not present in those who cannot see afar off and to him who has forgotten that he was purged from the sins of the past. The saints of God are a light that shines in the darkness until the dawning of the day that Christ returns and every knee bows and every tongue confesses that Jesus Christ is Lord to the glory of God the Father and the Daystar arise in the hearts of His people.

And so, all of Gods people in this final season begin to glorify God and they start by saying "Behold the Lamb of God who taketh away the sins of the world." For in the beginning was the Word and the Word was with God and the Word was God. He was in the beginning with God. And we know that all things exist through Him and not a single thing exists outside of Him. In Him is life and that life is the light of men. His people who have received Him are given authority to become the children of God. Behold unto us a Child is born, unto us a Son is given and the government is upon His shoulders and His name is wonderful, counselor, mighty God, Everlasting Father. He is the Prince of peace. Before me there was no God formed says the Lord. Nor shall there be after me, I, even I, am the Lord and besides me there is no Saviour.

I am the Alpha and the Omega, the first and the last and the living one and I became dead and behold I am alive forever and ever amen. And I have the keys of hell and death. I have seven stars in my right hand and I walk in the midst of the seven golden lamp stands. I say this to the overcomers, you will eat from the tree of life which is in the midst of my paradise. Do not fear what you are about to suffer, be faithful to death and I will give you the crown of life. To those who overcome I will give to eat of the hidden manna and will give to him a white stone and in that stone a new name will be written which no man knows except the one who receive it. I am the Son of God and my eyes are like a flame of fire and my feet like burnished metal and I say to the over-comers, hold fast that which you have until I come and I will give to you the power over nations. And I say to those who are not defiled, you will walk with me with garments of white and I will confess your name before my Father and before His angels.

I am He who is holy and true and I have the keys of David. I open and no one shuts, I shut and no one opens. Behold I have given you an open door and no one can shut it. For you have a little strength and have kept my words and have not denied my name. Hold fast so that no one takes your crown and I will make you a pillar in the temple of my God. Behold, I stand at the door and knock. If you hear my voice, open the door and we will dine together.

Behold that Lamb of God that taketh away the sins of the world. The creatures of heaven do not rest day or night but cry out "Holy, holy, holy, Lord God the Almighty who was and is and is to come." and they worship Him who lives forever and they throw their crowns before the throne saying "Oh Lord you are worthy to receive glory and honor and power." And a mighty angel shouts with a loud voice "Who is worthy to open the book and to loosen its seals." Behold the lion of the tribe of Judah. A Lamb, standing in the midst of the elders. He steps forward and takes the book from the right hand of Him sitting upon the throne. And the elders and the creatures fall down before the Lamb along with all the prayers of the saints. And they sang a new song. "You are worthy and were slain and have redeemed your people to God by your blood." People from all nations of the world gather around the throne with the angels and the elders and the creatures and they were without number and they sing "Worthy is the Lamb that was slain to receive power and riches and wisdom and strength and honor and glory and blessings."

And again the multitude which no man could number, dressed in white and with palms in their hands cried out "Salvation to our God who sits upon the throne and to the Lamb. Blessings and glory and wisdom and thanksgiving and honor and power and might be to our God forever and ever amen." And the tribulation saints washed in the blood of the Lamb serve before the throne of God day and night and God Himself dwells amongst them. And the Lamb who is in the midst of the throne feeds them and leads them to the fountains of living waters. And God wipes away all of their tears from their eyes.

Behold the Lamb of God that taketh away the sins of the world. And the heavens and earth passed away. And a great voice cried "Behold the tabernacle of God is with men and He dwells with them and they are His people and God is with them and He is their God. There is no more death nor mourning nor crying out, nor is there any more pain for these things have passed away." "It is done" says God, "I am the Alpha and the Omega, the Beginning and the end. To Him who thirsts I will give him the fountain of the waters of life freely. He who overcomes will inherit all things, I will be His God and He will be my Son. And in this place there is no temple for the Lord God Almighty is its temple, even the Lamb. And in this place there is no need for the sun, nor of the moon, for the glory of God illuminates it and its lamp is the Lamb."

Behold the Lamb of God who taketh away the sins of the world. From the throne of God and the Lamb proceed a pure river and its waters are the waters of life. And the Lamb says "Behold I am coming quickly and my reward is with Me. I am the Alpha and the Omega, the beginning and the ending, the First and the Last. I am the root and the offspring of David, the bright Morning Star. And the Spirit and the Bride say come. And let the one hearing say come. And let him who is thirsty come. Let him take of the waters of life freely. Yes I am coming quickly. The grace of the Lord Jesus Christ be with you all amen."

So brothers and sisters in Christ. It's time to gaze upon the wonder that is Jesus. Know who He is and who you are in Christ. His promises are yes and amen. He does not lie, the accuser of the brethren lies. Hold fast in these last days and glorify Him. All of His promises will come to pass and they are to you who know Him, they are to His remnant people. Go into battle with these glorious thoughts. We know in whom we serve, we know who we follow, we know some of what awaits us on the other side of glory. There is nothing in this world that compares to what the Word of God describes to those who overcome. It is a glorious vision and yet we know even this that "eye have not seen, nor ear heard, nor has it entered into the hearts of man the things that God has prepared for those who love Him."

There is a great multitude today who are desperately hungry and thirsty. All over the world the people dwell in great darkness and the darkness increases every day. Hell has opened its vaults and is beginning to spew forth evil with increasing speed and urgency because it knows its time is short. There is a desperate darkness coming and it is coming at us with alarming speed. Yet, as in the time of Noah, the world is ignorant of the impending disaster about to befall it. Like the children of Israel when Jesus says, "O

Jerusalem, Jerusalem, the one killing the prophets and stoning those who are sent to her, how often would I have gathered your children together, even as a hen gathers her chicks under her wings, and you would not!" Jesus wept because He knew that less than forty years after His death and resurrection that the whole system would come tumbling down.

The Temple would be destroyed and the Israelites would be no more as a nation and they had absolutely no idea. In those days, it was unimaginable that their Temple, their country, their way of life would be swept away and that they would be scattered to the four corners of the earth. It is equally unimaginable to so many that the church system that we know now, could and will be completely consumed by Babylon and turn on God's remnant children. Yet brothers and sisters, that is exactly what is to come as this great Babylonian whore church comes forward and worships the anti-christ. And despite all this, God's children will shine brightly in the darkest days the world has ever known. So full of the Spirit, walking in the presence of God. A blood bought remnant people whose desperate desire is to follow Him to Calvary and beyond, so that their eyes will see the Glory of the Living God cover the earth as the waters cover the sea. If persecution brings out the glory in the saints, if persecution takes place all over the world as it has never before, then so too will God's glory, a manifestation of Jesus, be revealed to the world. It will be clear to the world what they are rejecting and then the King shall appear. Oh for the day of His appearance when every eye shall see Him and every knee shall bow and every tongue confess that He is Lord to the glory of God.

17.

THE GLORY OF GOD.

What is the glory of God? We hear it used so often in Christian circles, but do you really know what that is? Is it just a description, an adjective, something to describe what you imagine God is like or what it is like to be in His presence? The truth is, the glory of God is God Himself. Wherever He is, then there is the glory. It is a dwelling place, it is His dwelling place. Moses had to put off his shoes because he was standing on holy ground. Now, was the ground holy before the Lord came? Was it holy after He left? What about the burning bush? When God inhabited the burning bush then the bush was God and could not be consumed by fire. Yet when the Lord left the bush was just a bush. Does God dwell in temples made by human hands? Is a church building holy? What is a building without the manifest presence of God? What is a person without the manifest presence of God operating in their lives? Where is the glory outside of the presence? How can the world see a manifestation of His presence if the manifestation of that presence cannot be seen in His children? We know that after Moses spent time in the manifest presence of God that his face actually glowed.

Before the Ark of the Covenant was brought into Solomon's temple, the temple was merely a human marvel, a wonder of the world to be sure, like the pyramids, yet simply a structure built by human hands. It is the presence of God represented by the Ark of the Covenant that made Solomon's temple special. When the ark took up residence in the heart of the temple then and only then was there a manifestation of God's glory.

2Ch 5:7 And the priests brought in the ark of the covenant of Jehovah to its place, to the Holy of Holies in the house, into the most holy place, under the wings of the cherubs. 2Ch 5:11 And it happened as the priests came out of the holy place, for all the priests present were sanctified, and did not wait by division.

You see brothers and sisters, when the ark was placed in the temple there was no division of the priests, they were as one. And the people were as one also

2Ch 5:12 And the Levitical singers, all of them of Asaph, of Heman, of Jeduthun, with their sons and their brothers, being clothed in white linen, having cymbals and with harps and lyres, stood at the east end of the altar, and with them a hundred and twenty priests sounding with trumpets,
*2Ch 5:13 **and they were as one** to the trumpeters and to the singers, to make one sound to be heard in praising and thanking Jehovah; and as they lifted up their voice with the trumpets and cymbals and instruments of music, and praised Jehovah, saying, For He is good, for His mercy endures forever, the house was filled with a cloud, the house of Jehovah,*
2Ch 5:14 so that the priests could not stand to minister because of the cloud, for the glory of Jehovah had filled the house of God!

You see brothers and sisters, when the people came together as one, without division and the ark took up its proper place in the holy of holies then God came down, His manifest presence filled the temple and the glory of God filled the house of God. When God brings His remnant people together, when He brings them out and they stand as one, with one mind and with one spirit then the glory of God will fall upon them for all the world to see. The glory of God will cover the earth as the waters cover the sea. There is no doubt that the glory of the first temple was an awesome thing, indeed it was a wonder of the ancient world. Solomon's temple was a marvel and without equal. It housed the Ark of the Covenant, which represented God's glory here on earth. Often the Shekinah glory of the Lord would rain down like fire and emanate in this glorious temple. Men from all over the known world would be drawn to this wonder and to the wisdom of its God ordained builder. The Queen of Sheba crossed many different lands to come and see what was going on in Jerusalem. This Temple would last for almost 400 years before being allowed to be destroyed by the Lord who allowed judgment to fall on Israel.

After 70 years, the Lord would bring His people back and they would lay the foundations to rebuild the temple. This temple was very much smaller than the original and of course there were still people alive who would have remembered the glory of the original temple. The people were discouraged by this and many other factors and had to be encouraged by God to rebuild, after the building had lain dormant for 16 years, that's a lot of years of discouragement. There would be no Ark of the Covenant, no Shekinah glory for this temple, yet little did the builders know that into this structure would walk, in the flesh, the King of Kings and the Lord of Lords.

This temple would hold the maker of heaven and earth and He would announce His mission to the world from this very spot, a great glory indeed. In this very temple, sin, desperately seeking for a hiding place, would be exposed by the light of the world. The bearers of this sin, the religious men of the day, were the last vestiges of a sin that had begun to be exposed by the Law and Moses. Now a greater One than Moses would enter right into the temple, the last place any one would look for sin, and expose it in the very heart of the hypocrisy of the "moral" men of the day. Seventy years after Jesus was born, once again the temple was destroyed. This time the former marvel of the ancient world would never rise again. Yet, each time the Lord would destroy a magnificent building, and replace it with something less, the glory revealed in the reduced surroundings would increase.

Now, in the final irony of this world, the temple would be rebuilt, but not with stones, not with bricks and mortar, not with inlaid gold, but with a people. And once again the Lord would increase the glory revealed. We, as true Christians, are the living stones, we are the temple of the living God. Jesus has entered into our hearts, not something built by men, and has taken up residence. The heart of Shekinah glory dwells in the center of each and every royal priest. His light, His love, His truth, His peace, His joy, His glory, His healing, His comfort, His power, His justice, His grace, His majesty, His deliverance and all that He is, burns at the very center of our being. This fire, the fire of the Holy Spirit, is housed in the temple of His choosing. Yet each of us are but one mere stone in the temple. And one stone does not a temple build. It is in the coming together of these stones that brings down the manifest glory of God corporately. God is bringing His stones together and assembling His new temple. He alone has shaped every stone. The master builder is building His very own temple.

And so, can we describe the glory? Jesus is the glory. Glory is the very essence of life itself. It's the breath a drowning man takes when he is one second away from death but somehow manages to burst through the waters and breathe. It's life itself. Glory is where all breath comes from. Glory is the oasis that the man in the desert stumbles upon having wandered without water to the point of death. Glory is where the living waters come from. Glory is when I have fallen and lay dying on the bloody battle-field of life and through the mist and the smoke of war rides the transfigured Christ. He carries me from there, through the gates of hell and death into the unbroken sunshine of a brand new dawn and I am renewed. Where He is, is glory, it is He and it is a dwelling place. A place where we are consciously one. To behold His glory is to be where He is.

Lord, when your glory comes down, when I walk with you where you are then my empty soul is filled and filled and filled to overflowing. I weep, I cry, I laugh, I love. I do this in your glory. I breathe glory into mortal lungs and I could run and never stop. I see glory with mortal eyes and suddenly your glory is everywhere. I truly see the beauty that you have created. Now I am aware of just how hungry I am for you and your glory. I am now ruined for everything else because I have seen the King and this world is such a poor second best, mere shades of grey in comparison to the light of your presence. I am so hungry, I stretch out my hands to heaven like a chick with open mouth waiting to be fed. To be fed by your glory is heaven's food. Every word from you is life to my soul. To consume and to be consumed. My mortal ears are opened and I hear heavenly choirs of angels sing unknown songs with notes that are beyond our grasp and resonate and penetrate my very DNA. This is the glory of God, complete oneness, wholeness. God is glory, glory is God and I dwell in it as I look into the face of Jesus, behold our God's glory is manifested and shines in the face of Christ our Lord. This is the spirit of Glory.

1Pe 4:14 If you are reviled for the name of Christ, you are blessed, because the Spirit of God and of glory rests on you

2Co 3:18 But we all, with our face having been unveiled, having beheld the glory of the Lord as in a mirror, are being changed into the same image from glory to glory, even as by the Lord's Spirit.

Act 7:55 But being full of the Holy Spirit, looking up intently into Heaven, he saw the glory of God, and Jesus standing at the right hand of God.

Eze 43:5 And the Spirit took me up and brought me into the inner chamber. And behold, the glory of Jehovah filled the house.

Joh 17:24 Father, I desire that those whom You have given Me, that they may be with Me where I am, that they may behold My glory which You have given Me, for You have loved Me before the foundation of the world.

The Unity of the Body is coming.

You cannot appease God by working for Him. You cannot become spiritual by keeping very active in some form of church activity, or the like. Gods cry and longing throughout the ages of eternity has been for a home, a resting place in a people made in His own image.... and God will not allow you to find rest in your own works. God will not allow you to rest until you find that rest in UNION WITH HIMSELF ALONE. (George Warnock, Feed My Sheep, pg 7)

You see what George is saying? God is looking for a home. He is looking to abide not just in the individual believer but in the Body of Christ that stands as one. No amount of work or activity can make this come to pass for unless the Lord builds the house then we labor in vain. What house does God want to abide in? He wants to abide in the Body of Christ. A collection of stones does not make a temple. Yes we need the stones and they must be cut from the quarry of this world and they must be taken and shaped.

Ye also, as lively stones, are built up a spiritual house, a holy priesthood, to offer up spiritual sacrifices, acceptable to God by Jesus Christ. (1Pe 2:5)

This is a painful but hard and vital part of the process. Yet, if the temple is to take shape then the stones must be taken to one place. They must be gathered together and transported to the proper location. What is the location of the temple of God that no human hand can build? The location is called unity.

*Neither pray I for these alone, but for them also which shall believe on me through their word; That they all may be one; as thou, Father, art in me, and I in thee, that they also may be one in us: that the world may believe that thou hast sent me. (*John 17:20-21)

Are we one brothers and sisters? Have we seen the fulfillment of the high priestly prayer of Jesus? Has the world seen this? Or, do they see the exact opposite? You see Jesus requires the unity of His people as a witness to the world.

But ye are a chosen generation, a royal priesthood, an holy nation, a peculiar people; that ye should shew forth the praises of him who hath called you out of darkness into his marvellous light (1 Pet 2:9)

Is this what the world sees? Do they see a holy people, a peculiar people, a people who is not like them? Christ will not return until we are a witness to the world *.This gospel of the kingdom shall be*

*preached in all the world for a witness unto all nations; and then
shall the end come"* (Matthew 24:14).

God is gathering His stones together in this day. He is calling His
priesthood to one place that they may show forth His praises. Now
what does that phrase "shew forth," mean? It means to publish, to
announce, to put front and center. Let me argue that we have never
seen this unity but let me further argue that what Christ wants
Christ gets. When Jesus prays to His Father that *"they all may be
one"* then I put it to you that this will come to pass not just
figuratively, for if it were simply figuratively then how could that
be a witness to the world? Will Satan attempt to counterfeit this
unity prior to the Lord revealing the true Church? Certainly he has
already and will continue to until it culminates in the great whore
church. Consider the words of Pope Francis recently and take heed
of a coming counterfeit unity by the religions of the world....

*Our communities continue to experience divisions, which are a
scandal. There is no other word for it: the divisions between
Christians are a scandal...because they used Christ's name to
separate themselves from others within the Christian community.
But the name of Christ creates communion and unity, not division!
Baptism and the Cross are central elements in our common
Christian discipleship. Divisions, on the other hand, weaken the
credibility and effectiveness of our commitment to evangelization.*
Pope Francis – General Audience – 22 January 2014

You see brothers and sisters, Satan knows that the Lord is bringing
the remnant saints together for the end-days persecution so that
they may be one and be a witness to the world and then Christ
comes. And that old usurper and father of lies is already putting
into place his own unity of "believers" for the end days that will be
the deadliest enemy of the Royal Priesthood. The once born man
understands what it means to work together in unity, to strive
together to reach new heights. This is the symbolism of the tower
of Babel where the brotherhood of man worked together to create
their own monument to their own greatness. God's monument to
men are built by God's own hand and He inhabits what He builds,

He does not inhabit what men build. *Howbeit the most High dwelleth not in temples made with hands; as saith the prophet, Heaven is my throne, and earth is my footstool: what house will ye build me? saith the Lord: or what is the place of my rest?* (Acts 7:48-49)

God is calling forth a people who will walk in the Truth and in Unity and be a resting place, a house to dwell in for Himself. It is prophesied by Jesus Himself in Matt 24:14 and in John 17: 20-21 and will most certainly come to pass. Perhaps you look at the landscape of Christendom and think that this is an impossibility? Yes indeed, with men and with the work of men this is impossible and has proven to be so, but with God all things are possible and when He says a thing will come to pass then it shall come to pass. Be encouraged brothers and sisters, God is at work and He is working with "lively stones," all over the world. Prior to judgment, God called all the animals of the world to one place, to the ark of Noah. Now how did they come? How did they know to come and where to come to? If God can speak to animals and draw them together from all over the planet, He can and will speak to His people prior to the last judgment and He will bring them together and they will be a witness to the world and then He will come.

18.

The failed system of the church

This final chapter of the book will look at the failed and fatally flawed system of church that we have labored under for centuries. I know that this is a controversial subject and I have lost friends over this but I must speak what the Lord has laid upon my heart. It is quite an audacious thing to say that the very system that most of Christendom labors under is un-biblical and flawed but there it is, that is what I believe. The mere fact that it has existed in some form or fashion for countless centuries in no way legitimizes it. If it did, then the Catholic Church would be the most legitimate church that we have. It seems plain enough that in Scripture, Christians met in their homes and their very homes became places of worship, houses of prayer if you like. The outside world saw life in these people, saw love in these people and God Himself added to them daily. Think about all the church programs that are designed to get new members or to somehow stop the "revolving door" and keep the folks who come and visit. Yet the early believers had no such programs.

What led people to the truth was the very life in those who represented it. A burning love and passion for Jesus. They had no desire to bring folks to their particular house, or tell people that they must hear their particular teacher or pastor, no their singular obsession and passion was for the one who radically transformed their lives and it was now no longer them that lived but Christ lived in them. Therefore they were not afraid to die for Jesus, in fact, the early Church counted it as a great honor and thanked God that they were counted worthy to suffer for Him. This was the life of Christ burning in their bones, coursing through their veins, it completely dominated their whole lives, their life was about His life in them and this drew others to Jesus. God Himself was given all the honor and the glory for the drawing of others to Himself as of course it should be. Consider the words of T.A.Sparks.............................

The Lord has not called upon us to form churches. That is not our business. Would to God men had recognized the fact! A very different situation would obtain today from what exists, if that had been recognized. It is the Lord Who expands His Church, Who governs its growth. What we have to do is to live in the place of His appointment in the power of His resurrection. If, in the midst of others, the Lord can get but two of His children, in whom His Life is full and free, to live on the basis of that Life, and not to seek to gather others to themselves or to get them to congregate together on the basis of their acceptance of certain truths or teaching, but simply to witness to what Christ means and is to them, then He has an open way....

The Church is not increased by your going and taking a building and trying to get people to come to it, and to your meetings, and then forming them, by a church roll, into a local church. That is not the way. Growth is by Life, and this, to begin with, may be by the entering into Life of but one soul, and then after a long waiting time of another; or it may be more rapid. But the point is that it is increase because of Life. That is the growth of the Church. For the growth of His Church, the Lord must have Life channels, Life centers. I believe that, given a Life center, sooner or later one of two things will happen, that it will be abundantly manifest that Christ is fully and finally rejected there, or else there will be an adding, a growth. There is tremendous power in Life, and the Life of the Lord either kills or quickens. It depends on the attitude taken toward it. He is a savor of Life unto Life, or of death unto death. Things can never remain neutral.
(T.A.Sparks)

You see brothers and sisters, life attracts life. And it is these lives that form the Body of Christ. It is not our religious clubs or denominations that form the Body of Christ, it is the life of Christ in His own that constitute the Body. The Body is scattered throughout Christendom and for the most is to be found in the religious clubs and denominations that make up Christendom today. Yet it was not always that way and it will not always be that way, indeed, with Christ at the door, there is a calling by God on His people to come out. In all the lost centuries of Catholic domination by denomination, rightly called the dark ages, there was a Pilgrim church, operating outside of the authority of the ruling religious establishment. This is what kept the light burning in the world through the dark ages, this was the Body of Christ. All attempts at keeping any kind of fire burning within religious establishments always failed in the end. Ultimately religion must have the authority and for Christ's own, there is one head of the Church and that is Christ. Listen to what Broadbent says in the book "The Pilgrim Church." ....

" The histories of the monks and the friars shows that if a spiritual movement can be kept within the confines of the Roman Catholic Church or any similar system, it is doomed and must be dragged down to the level of that which it sought originally to reform. It purchases exemption from persecution at the cost of its life. Francis of Assisi and Peter Waldo were both laid hold of by the same teaching of the Lord and yielded themselves to Him with uttermost devotion. In each case the example set and the teaching given gained the hearts of large numbers and affected their whole manner of life. The likeness turned to contrast when the one was accepted and the other rejected by the organized religion of Rome. The inward relation to the Lord may have remained the same, but the working out of the two lives differed widely. The Franciscans being absorbed into the Roman system, helped to blind men to it, while Waldo and his band of preachers directed multitudes of souls to the Scriptures, where they learned to draw for themselves fresh and inexhaustible supplies from the "wells of salvation." (The Pilgrim Church, pg 117)

You see brothers and sisters, those outside of the religious structures were able to draw "inexhaustible supplies from the wells of salvation." It may have looked to the world that these groups of pilgrim gatherings that had taken themselves outside of the religious system would flounder due to lack of leadership and authority and resources that the Catholic Church brought to bear, but the truth was quite the opposite. God is well able to look after His children wherever they may be and He can produce springs in the desert and cause manna to fall from the heavens as the saints make their way home to the Promised Land, to that new Heavenly

Jerusalem. It is a narrow and difficult path of course and we can wonder oftentimes why the wicked seem to prosper and live lives of relative ease and comfort, but it is the necessary way home. We may not have ease and comfort in this world and those of the religious persuasion may sometimes seem to have many comforts here, but our journey is an eternal one, our Kingdom is not of this world. We are merely passing through, sojourners and gypsies to the world, yet God's ambassadors, pilgrims in a foreign land, looking to journey home. The travails of the road may seem very difficult sometimes, very lonely and difficult, but this will only make our arrival home all the sweeter.

Listen to what Tozer says as he cries out for forgiveness for his own participation in a religious system that has "robbed " Christ of any true authority in the churches and has relegated Him to but a mere figurehead, a name to rubber stamp man-made programs.........

"If I know my own heart it is love alone that moves me to write this. What I write here is not the sour ferment of a mind agitated by contentions with my fellow Christians. There have been no such contentions. I have not been abused, mistreated or attacked by anyone. Nor have these observations grown out of any unpleasant experiences that I have had in my association with others. My relations with my own church as well as with Christians of other denominations have been friendly, courteous and pleasant. My grief is simply the result of a condition which I believe to be almost universally prevalent among the churches.

I think also that I should acknowledge that I am myself very much involved in the situation I here deplore. As Ezra in his mighty prayer of intercession included himself among the wrongdoers, so do I. "O my God, I am ashamed and blush to lift up my face to thee, my God: for our iniquities are increased over our head, and our trespass is grown up unto the heavens" (9:6). Any hard word spoken here against others must in simple honesty return upon my own head. I too have been guilty. This is written with the hope that we all may turn unto the Lord our God and sin no more against Him.

Let me state the cause of my burden. It is this: Jesus Christ has today almost no authority at all among the groups that call themselves by His name. By these I mean not the Roman Catholics, nor the liberals, nor the various quasi-Christian cults. I do mean Protestant churches generally, and I include those that protest the loudest that they are in spiritual descent from our Lord and His apostles, namely the evangelicals." (Tozer)

He takes no time to discount the Catholics and the liberals, Jehovahs and Mormons, for it should be apparent to all that they do not have Christ as their authority, no he takes direct aim at Protestant churches in general and evangelicals in particular. Their system of churches is such that the life of Christ must be snuffed out in favor of the traditions and doctrines of men. Again, saints are scattered throughout all of these churches, good men and women laboring under an unbiblical system that always snuffs out the life of Christ, the authority of Christ, the pre-eminence of Christ. In the end it is done in favor of their own authority, their own traditions and their own survival. Notice that in most non-denominational churches, the pre-eminence passes from Christ to the preacher/teacher/pastor. We are living in the days of the personality cult where the man or the woman is lifted up as they rob and steal from the Word of God for their own fame and enrichment.

Now the coming of the end of ages is upon us brothers and sisters. Christ is at the door. Great darkness has covered the land and gross darkness is almost upon us. There is a gathering storm that is brewing and the likes of it has never been seen before. Great persecution has come against God's people in many parts of the world and shall now come against the saints in the west who have been living in relative peace and safety for some time. We have been living at ease in Babylon but Babylon will take back what it has given. Saints in the west will lose everything in the coming persecution prior to Christ returning.

Those of the religious system whose hearts truly belong to the world and not to Christ will turn upon the saints as the saints begin to draw back from gross worldliness. The saints will be compelled to leave their comfort behind in a system that has done all of their studying for them, their worshipping for them, a system where they were only truly compelled to give their tithes and offerings and then sit silent as spectators while they were taught and entertained by paid professionals. This may seem like a disaster but it will be the finest thing that ever happened to the Body of Christ. Their unity, prophesied by Jesus in John 17, will finally begin to materialize and it will be forged in the fires of blood and persecution. Ungodly, un-biblical denominational divisions will begin to evaporate for the saints as they come together and glorify Christ and witness to the world. Listen to what Spurgeon says of his own Baptist denomination back in the 1850s as he looks forward to such a time...........................

"I say of the Baptist name, let it perish, but let Christ's name last forever. I look forward with pleasure to the day when there will not be a Baptist living. I hope they will soon be gone. You will say, Why? .... But, I say, let even England's name perish; let her be merged in one great brotherhood; let us have no England, and no France, and no Russia, and no Turkey, but let us have Christendom; and I say heartily from my soul, let nations and national distinctions perish, but let Christ's name last for ever." (C.H. Spurgeon, The Eternal Name, Sermon, May 27th, 1855).

John Wesley said, *"Would to God that all party names, and unscriptural phrases and forms which have divided the Christian world, were forgot... I should rejoice if the very name (Methodist) might never be mentioned more, but be buried in eternal oblivion" (The Works of John Wesley).*

Frank Bartleman said this of the pentecostal move of the early 1900's: *"The truth must be told. Azusa began to fail the Lord also, early in her history. God showed me one day that they were going to organize... He had me get up and warn them against making a party spirit of the Pentecostal work. The baptized saints were to remain one body... Surely a party spirit cannot be Pentecostal. There can be no divisions in a true Pentecost. To formulate a separate body is but to advertise our failure, as people of God. It proves to the world that we cannot get along together, rather than causing them to believe in our salvation. '...That they all may be one... that the world may believe..." (Jn. 17.21)" (Frank Bartleman, Azusa Street).*

In the Spurgeon quote, he uses his beloved England as an analogy of all the various sects and denominations of Christianity. He would see them all swallowed up for the glory of Christ's name and that name alone lifted up. All other names will fail in the coming persecution. It is only by being identified by Christ and Christ alone that one will stand in the evil day. For in that evil day only those churches and denominations who have acquiesced to the evil authorities will be able to exist. My own prayer would be that all would stand for Christ in that day and be willing to suffer and count it a worthy thing to suffer for the name of Jesus and for that and under that name alone. The sad truth is that already so many churches and denominations have fallen at the first hurdle and yet we are merely in the birth pang stages. As the intensity increases, more and more will fall away from the truth. Yet the Body of Christ, the true Church of Christ will come forward and be counted. They will stand in unity under that name which is above every name. Their light will shine greatly as the greatest darkness the world has ever known engulfs the world in gross wickedness and violence. Like gold in the hottest fire, it will simply purify the saints.

A possible scenario for end time events

This subject can be very difficult to approach today because there have been so many crazy people claiming when the end of the world would happen. The below scenario reckons on the saints going through the great tribulation or at least a part of it. Therefore there is no particular day or hour that is looked for, rather a season, birth pangs if you like. We are told by Jesus that we should be able to discern the signs of the times, not the day nor the hour of His return. In any event, most Peoples of the world and the church have a difficult time imagining a time where Christians would be hunted down and killed for the mere fact of being Christian. They may be able to imagine this in a Muslim world setting, but not in the West. I do not claim that the scenario below is prophetic, I merely wish to show you a logical procession of events that could lead to a world-wide persecution of the true saints.

I think we may all agree that Jesus is coming relatively soon. Where we may disagree is on the subject of rapture. Let's assume there is no rapture and Jesus is coming soon, then the saints will go through the great tribulation. The Scriptures tells us that it will be worse than anything that has ever happened before in history, in fact the Lord must shorten those days for the elects sake or we would all be dead.

Just 70 years ago, in the heart of educated and cultured Europe, in a country that pronounced itself to be Christian, an evil man arose and in six short years, killed six million Jews for the mere fact of being Jewish. He shoved them into gas chambers and then burned them in furnaces, men, women and children, sparing none. Now this is not some Biblical genocide from the ancient world, this is something that happened just 70 years ago. Now what kind of events would need to unfold for the world to turn on Christians and for there to be a coming together of the world religions into one religion?

Let's say tomorrow there is an attack by Muslim extremists on multiple cities. New York, Washington, London, Paris Rome and Moscow are hit simultaneously with nuclear suitcase bombs. Rather than the three thousand dead of 9/11, there is one hundred thousand dead in each city. The world is repulsed and is brought together because of this great tragedy. Fundamentalists of all stripes are universally condemned and outlawed. To state publicly that there is only one true religion, only one way to heaven, becomes illegal. Such people are denounced as those who have caused all the troubles in the world. They are seen as a cancer on society which society must rid itself of.

So society gives them a chance to renounce such beliefs. At the same time, the major religions of the world have a summit. Islam, Christianity and the Jewish faith come together for a summit in Rome. Pope Francis leads the summit because he is universally respected. When the meeting is over they announce that they can all trace their roots back to Abraham. They say they all worship the same God just in different ways. They announce that there are multiple roads to heaven and that to say otherwise is merely hate speech. They agree to drop Jesus and Mohammed from their literature and only speak in terms of God and His prophets, agreeing to stand upon what they agree on and bringing a historic unity that will usher in a new day, a new order for the world where there is equality for all.

The vast majority of the world hail this as a great turning point and rejoice in it. A small minority resist it and in the shadow of the multiple hundreds and thousands of deaths, the world hates them with a perfect hatred. They hate them more than the Germans hated the Jews. The minority cannot find work and are ultimately arrested for continuing to "share the Gospel." While they are a minority, they are still in the millions and camps are set up to imprison them because the prison system cannot contain them. An ever-growing hatred by the general public and resentment that they have to be fed and kept eventually leads to the decision to make it a capital offense punishable by death to be a fundamental Christian.

If I had time and space, I could weave into that scenario the rise of the anti-christ who orchestrates all of those events and performs signs and wonders and miracles in front of the whole world to legitimize what he and the Pope and the religious leaders are teaching and saying about the minority, the remnant who refused to bow their knees to such a world religion. I want you to imagine such a man, before the cameras of the world, healing a man blind from birth, or raising a man from the dead. The whole world will follow after such a man, and the world religious leaders who are now one would verify that he is in fact, God returned.

This is just one possible scenario of end time events. I wanted to show you that we are but one catalyst away from everything changing overnight. So many of the building blocks are already in place and it is time for the saints to arise from their slumbers. We must be prepared in our hearts and minds and Spirits for what is to come. I have tried to lay out in this book fundamental truths and the fact that God is calling His remnant people. I pray that even if you do not agree with everything that I have written, or even if you do not agree with most of what I have written, that you were still blessed in the reading of this book. And so here is my challenge to all who have made it to this point in the book. I want you " to stand."

To Stand In The Evil Day.

Isa 7:9b If you do not stand firm in your faith, you will not stand at all.

The Anglican Church has confirmed and is affirming homosexual marriage and the ordination of practicing homosexual ministers. This extends to the church in Scotland and Ireland and France and all throughout Europe. And of course right here in the States many of the mainline denominations have already given themselves over to this gross error even before the Supreme court rules on the issue.

Now the question must be asked, why then do genuine saints stay with such corrupt organizations? Indeed that must be a question that every saint around the world who identifies themselves under the name and the banner of such organizations must ask themselves. Is it misplaced loyalty? Is it merely because of tradition? Is it a fundamental lack of understanding of just what the Scriptures are referring to when it speaks of the Body of Christ and the unity of the Body? My question would be to any saint found within the walls of any organizations that sanctify and solemnize homosexuality " where is your loyalty to the Truth?" Are you so divided in heart and mind that you can overlook this? What next? If they were to strip the Lord Jesus of His Son-ship would you still stay? If they were to advocate that there are many paths to heaven would you stay?

Now I am not picking on homosexuality in particular. There are many sins of which these denominations have overlooked and then ultimately embraced. My argument would be that if this is not the straw that breaks the camels back then the camels back is not going to be broken. It stands in such violation to the word of God that the people who embrace such error are truly without excuse. I believe God Himself is exposing the very underpinnings of these institutions. So therefore, if God is speaking are you listening? The Scripture above reminds us of a fundamental truth " If you do not stand firm in your faith, you will not stand at all." When Judah was face with destruction and the hearts of her people were shaken like the wind shakes the trees then they are advised to stand firm in your faith or you shall not stand at all. This, I believe, is the admonition by the Lord to His people today. Stand firm, do not be moved by the cultural winds of the world that are blowing with hurricane force for if you do not you shall not stand.

God is compelling His saints to stand firm. Now is the time to take a stand. Now is the time to be fully identified, not with a denomination, but with Christ alone and His Body. His Body is not corrupted, so shall you corrupt your own body by staying within the confines of a church that has overthrown the Word of God? Shall you not come out from with her? In 2 Cor Paul asks these questions and they demand answers. What fellowship has righteousness with unrighteousness? What communion has light with darkness? What agreement has the temple of the Lord with idols? What fellowship has he that believes with those who do not? Does Christ have fellowship with idols? Therefore Paul exhorts to " come out from among them and be separate....and touch not the unclean thing, and I will receive you."

Now, every genuine saint, in this evil day, must discern for himself or herself if what they are a part of is unclean. If they determine that it is, then they must decide if they will stand firm in the faith and follow Jesus outside the camp or stay and be caught up in the great falling away. In this day, one will either stand firm in the faith or they will not stand at all. Yes, it is that dire. We are told in Ephesians 6 to take unto you the whole armor of God, that ye may be able to withstand in the evil day, and having done all, to stand. In the day in which we live and the darker days ahead it will not be about great ministries and so on, the challenge to the Body of Christ will simply be to "stand."

The questions are "will you stand firm in your faith?" "Will you stand upon the Word?" " Will you stand with Jesus and be identified with none other?" " Will you stand for the Truth?" You see, the great falling away which we are presently in the midst of is like a mighty river that is flowing with great strength. It has been wide up until now but the banks which contain this river are getting narrower and narrower and the downhill descent is getting steeper and steeper. Now when this happens in the natural then the current of the river accelerates to such a point that nothing can stand, it will sweep everything off of its feet. Yet praise God, if we take ourselves out of this river then God will receive us when we reject the unclean thing. He has His own river whose streams make glad the people of God.

When we stand in this river, though the waters of the world roar on their way down into hell, and the mountains shake and the stars seem to fall from the sky, there is a tabernacle, a dwelling place for the children of God. His presence is a refuge and our strength in this present time. For those who stand upon the Word when all the world is falling, stand in the very tabernacle of God, the heart of the Father and they are safe. He alone is the Holy ground upon which we stand. Psalm 18 says *You enlarge my steps under me, And my feet have not slipped.* And again in Psalm 31 *and you have not delivered me into the hand of the enemy; you have set my feet in a broad place.* And finally in 2 Sam *22 Thou hast enlarged my steps under me; so that my feet did not slip.*

God's people shall stand in this evil day, and having done all, having stood firm in the faith they shall stand. Stand as a testimony to the power and the glory of the one who gives us strength and becomes the very ground upon which we stand, Jesus. We shall not be ashamed of that name which is above every name. There is power in our un-ashamedness for the Truth of the Gospel and the living reality of the Christ who dwells in us. Must we lose all for Christ's sake? Very possibly in the world in which we now find ourselves. Yet for those who are willing to make that stand, take that loss, they will count it as nothing, as rubbish rather they will rejoice that they find themselves standing in Him, the very river of God that makes glad the hearts of His children and refreshes them and restores them and empowers them. Stand firm, our Lord is at the door.

ABOUT THE AUTHOR

Frank McEleny was born and raised in Greenock, Scotland. He and his wife moved to the States when he was 26.He gave his life to Jesus at the age of 27. He attended Bible School in the United States . He writes for "A Call to the Remnant," and has published over 700 articles. He was the moderator of a national prayer call for revival for two years and has been involved in various aspects of the revival ministry. He has helped moderate revival conferences and also has been a prayer co-ordinator. He initiated and helped organize the Greenock Revival Conference in 2008. He was ordained in 2013 by a small church in Oklahoma. He is also a published poet, publishing one hundred and fifty poems in the book entitled " A Poem for Every Psalm." He also writes hymns and songs, many of the songs have been recorded. His website is www.acalltotheremnant.com. He currently lives with his wife and grown son, who has Down Syndrome, in Kansas where he has lived for more than twenty years and works as a Real Estate Agent. You can find many of his poems at https://www.facebook.com/PoemsFromFrank

Made in the USA
Middletown, DE
14 April 2018